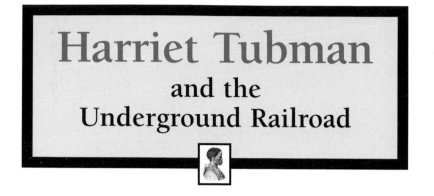

Harriet Tubman

and the
Underground Railroad

Other titles in this series:

A Dream Deferred: The Jim Crow Era

The Fight Renewed: The Civil Rights Movement

Forty Years of Medical Racism: The Tuskegee Experiments

The Harlem Renaissance

A History of Free Blacks in America

Marcus Garvey and the Back to Africa Movement

A Peculiar Institution: Slavery in the Plantation South

The Quest for Freedom: The Abolitionist Movement

Ray Charles and the Birth of Soul

Harriet Tubman
and the
Underground Railroad

Lucent Library of Black History

Louise Chipley Slavicek

LUCENT BOOKS

An imprint of Thomson Gale, a part of The Thomson Corporation

Detroit • New York • San Francisco • San Diego • New Haven, Conn.
Waterville, Maine • London • Munich

For more information, contact
Lucent Books
27500 Drake Rd.
Farmington Hills, MI 48331-3535
Or you can visit our Internet site at http://www.gale.com

LIBRARY OF CONGRESS CATALOGING-IN-PUBLICATION DATA

Slavicek, Louise Chipley, 1956–
    Harriet Tubman and the underground railroad / by Louise Chipley Slavicek.
        p. cm. — (Lucent library of Black history)
    Includes bibliographical references and index.
    ISBN 1-59018-927-2 (hard cover : alk. paper) 1. Tubman, Harriet, 1820?-1913—Juvenile literature. 2. Slaves—United States—Biography—Juvenile literature. 3. African American women—Biography—Juvenile literature. 4. Underground railroad—Juvenile literature. I. Title. II. Series.
    E444.T82S53 2006
    973.7'115092—dc22
                                                                    2005033932

Printed in the United States of America

Contents

Foreword   6

Introduction
Heroine of the Underground Railroad   8

Chapter One
Born into Slavery   12

Chapter Two
"Liberty, or Death"   29

Chapter Three
Conductor on the Underground Railroad   46

Chapter Four
"The Slaves Call Her Moses"   62

Chapter Five
"To Take Care of My People"   76

Notes   94
Timeline   97
For Further Reading   98
Index   100
Picture Credits   103
About the Author   104

Foreword

It has been more than five hundred years since Africans were first brought to the New World in shackles, and over 140 years since slavery was formally abolished in the United States. Over 50 years have passed since the fallacy of "separate but equal" was obliterated in the American courts, and some forty years since the watershed Civil Rights Act of 1965 guaranteed the rights and liberties of all Americans, especially those of color. Over time, these changes have become celebrated landmarks in American history. In the twenty-first century, African American men and women are politicians, judges, diplomats, professors, deans, doctors, artists, athletes, business owners, and home owners. For many, the scars of the past have melted away in the opportunities that have been found in contemporary society. Observers such as Peter N. Kirsanow, who sits on the U.S. Commission of Civil Rights, point to these accomplishments and conclude, "The growing black middle class may be viewed as proof that most of the civil rights battles have been won."

In spite of these legal victories, however, prejudice and inequality have persisted in American society. In 2003, African Americans comprised just 12 percent of the nation's population, yet accounted for 44 percent of its prison inmates and 24 percent of its poor. Racially motivated hate crimes continue to appear on the pages of major newspapers in many American cities. Furthermore, many African Americans still experience either overt or muted racism in their daily lives. A 1996 study undertaken by Professor Nancy Krieger of the Harvard School of Public Health, for example, found that 80 percent of the African American participants reported having experienced racial discrimination in one or more settings, including at work or school, applying for housing and medical care, from the police or in the courts, and on the street or in a public setting.

It is for these reasons that many believe the struggle for racial equality and justice is far from over. These episodes of discrimination threaten to shatter the illusion that America has completely overcome its racist past, causing many black Americans to become increasingly frustrated and confused. Scholar and writer Ellis Cose has described this splintered state in the following way: "I have done everything I was supposed to do. I have stayed out of trouble with the law, gone to the right schools, and worked myself nearly to death. What more do they want? Why in God's name won't they accept me as a full human being?" For Cose and others, the struggle for equality and justice has yet to be fully achieved.

In many subtle yet important ways the traumatic experiences of slavery and segregation continue to inform the way race is discussed and experienced in the twenty-first century. Indeed, it is possible that America will always grapple with the fallout from its distressing past. Ulric Haynes, dean of the Hofstra University School of Business has said, "Perhaps race will always matter, given the historical circumstances under which we came to this country." But studying this past and understanding how it contributes to present-day dialogues about race and history in America is a critical component of contemporary education. To this end, the Lucent Library of Black History offers a thorough look at the experiences that have shaped the black community and the American people as a whole. Annotated bibliographies provide readers with ideas for further research, while fully documented primary and secondary source quotations enhance the text. Each book in the series explores a different episode of black history; together they provide students with a wealth of information as well as launching points for further study and discussion.

Heroine of the Underground Railroad

The Underground Railroad is not only one of the most dramatic but also one of the best-known themes in U.S. history. Most Americans are familiar with the secret network of black and white volunteers that developed during the decades leading up to the Civil War to help fugitive slaves from the South reach sanctuary in Canada or the free states of the North. Yet probably very few could name even a single Underground Railroad agent, with one notable exception: the great black heroine of the legendary freedom line, Harriet Tubman.

Born into slavery on Maryland's Eastern Shore about 1821, as a child Harriet Tubman endured brutal beatings from a series of abusive masters and mistresses and as an adolescent nearly died after being struck in the head by a white overseer. At some point during her young adulthood, she learned of the clandestine, interracial organization dedicated to assisting runaways known as the Underground Railroad. She began to believe there might actually be a way out of her misery. When she was in her late twenties, after hearing that her owner intended to sell her to out-of-state slave traders, Tubman finally turned to her contacts in the Underground to help her make the perilous journey north to freedom.

The Underground Railroad's Most Celebrated Agent

When she first crossed the border into free Pennsylvania in 1849, Harriet Tubman became one of perhaps a thousand slaves to escape the chains of bondage that year in North America. Historians estimate that up to fifty thousand African Americans fled the slave states and territories from the beginning of the nineteenth century until the outbreak of the Civil War in 1861. Although many fugitives made their way to freedom entirely on their own, countless others relied on the men and women of the Underground Railroad to guide and safeguard them on their long, hazardous treks north. Running away required enormous courage: If recaptured, slaves faced horrific punishments that included shackling, branding, mutilating, and near-fatal whippings. Yet

The Underground Railroad was a network of volunteers who helped slaves escape to the North. In this illustration, freed slaves arrive in Baltimore, Maryland.

Charles T. Webber's 1893 painting "The Underground Railroad" depicts a group of fugitive slaves being helped toward freedom.

providing assistance of any kind to a runaway also took guts. After the passage of the harsh Fugitive Slave Act of 1850, heavy fines and lengthy terms of imprisonment confronted Underground agents caught in the act of aiding and abetting fugitive slaves. And for those intrepid few like Harriet Tubman who, upon securing their own liberty, returned to the land of their enslavers to help others reach freedom, the risks were even greater.

Many ex-slaves worked for the Underground Railroad in the free states and over the border in Canada. They provided shelter, clothes, food, or other assistance to recent escapees. Only a handful, however, jeopardized their hard-earned liberty to escort runaways personally out of the South. Harriet Tubman made more than a dozen trips to the slave states of Maryland, Delaware, and Virginia between 1850 and 1860. She led as many as two hundred men, women, and children to freedom and was unquestionably the most famous and effective of that elite group of fugitive guides, or conductors. Indeed, many scholars believe that Tubman shepherded more slaves northward than any other

Underground Railroad conductor in the history of the network, whether black or white, slave born or freeborn.

Aside from her remarkable success in spiriting runaways out of slave territory, what made Harriet Tubman stand out from the rest of her colleagues in the Underground Railroad was her gender. Many scholars, including her recent biographer Catherine Clinton, believe that Tubman was not only the first but also the only female conductor on the Liberty Line. After the Civil War erupted, Tubman redirected her antislavery efforts to assisting the Union cause as a nurse, scout, and spy. Thus, she achieved another first for her sex by becoming the very first American woman to lead an armed military expedition into enemy territory in the Combahee River raid of 1863.

Unquestionably the Underground Railroad's most famous volunteer during her own lifetime, since her death in 1913, Harriet Tubman has become nothing less than a symbol for the entire network. More than that of any other Underground operative, her personal chronicle of extraordinary courage, resourcefulness, and self-sacrifice would shape later generations' understanding of the clandestine organization. Owing to its secretive nature, modern scholars have struggled to recreate the Underground Railroad's activities and significance during the critical decades leading up to the Civil War. Thanks to the network's covert character as well, the story of the Underground Railroad has become the stuff of legend. By examining the real-life motivations and deeds of the Underground Railroad's central heroine, Harriet Tubman, historians have begun to separate myth from fact and gain new insights.

Chapter One

Born into Slavery

Harriet Tubman was born into slavery on a Maryland plantation roughly two hundred years after the first shipload of African slaves landed in Jamestown, Virginia, in 1619. The hardships Harriet experienced growing up enslaved on Maryland's Eastern Shore were typical of those endured by hundreds of thousands of other African American children in the antebellum South. Most slaves endured a crushing workload, brutal punishments, and the constant fear that family members could be sold at any moment.

Harriet Tubman's Uncertain Beginnings

Little is known about Harriet Tubman's earliest years. Even Harriet's date of birth is uncertain, since her owner did not bother to record it in the plantation ledgers. The failure of her master to document her arrival into the world was hardly unusual. Slaves were thought of as chattel (movable property), much like cattle and other livestock, and few slave owners kept written accounts of their births or deaths. Harriet thought that she was born in 1825 and testified to that effect in court on several occasions. Yet the birth year listed on her death certificate is 1815, fully a decade earlier. Most of Harriet Tubman's recent biographers, however, accept neither of these dates as accurate. Instead, they place Harriet's date of birth sometime between 1820 and 1822.

Just as Harriet Tubman's birth year is open to speculation, historians can only make educated guesses regarding the exact location of her birth. Scholars do know that Harriet was a native of Dorchester County in Maryland's Eastern Shore. The area was a fertile and densely wooded land bounded by Chesapeake Bay on the west, Delaware on the east, and Pennsylvania to the north. But they cannot say with any certainty where Harriet Tubman's mother, Rit (short for Harriet), was living and working at the time of her daughter's birth. Until recently, most of her biographers assumed that Harriet was born near the village of Bucktown on

Harriet Tubman grew up on a Maryland plantation in a slave house like this one.

the plantation of her mother's owner, Mary Pattison Brodess. However, the most current evidence indicates that she was probably born near the town of Tobacco Stick about ten miles (16km) northwest of the Brodess estate, on the estate of Anthony Thompson, the owner of her father, Ben Ross.

"I Do Not Remember to Have Ever Met a Slave Who Could Tell of His Birthday"

In his 1845 autobiography, *Narrative of the Life of Frederick Douglass, An American Slave*, the celebrated African American abolitionist Frederick Douglass bemoaned the fact that the vast majority of slaves in the antebellum South did not know their own birth dates:

I have no accurate knowledge of my age, never having seen any authentic record containing it. By far the larger part of the slaves know as little of their ages as horses know of theirs, and it is the wish of most masters within my knowledge to keep their slaves thus ignorant. I do not remember to have ever met a slave who could tell of his birthday. They seldom come nearer to it than planting-time, harvest-time, cherry-time, spring-time, or fall-time. A want of information concerning my own was a source of unhappiness to me even during childhood. The white children could tell their ages. I could not tell why I ought to be deprived of the same privilege.

Frederick Douglass was a noted leader in the antislavery movement.

Frederick Douglass, *Narrative of the Life of Frederick Douglass, An American Slave*. 1845. Reprint, New York: Penguin, 1982, p. 47.

Harriet Tubman's parents likely met for the first time in 1803, when Anthony Thompson married Mary Brodess, a recent widow, and Rit's mistress moved from her late husband's Bucktown farm to Thompson's wooded estate on the banks of the Little Choptank River. A few years after their owners' households were joined by marriage, Ben, a timber inspector, and Rit, a cook and nursemaid to Mary's young son, Edward Brodess, also wed. Rit and Ben Ross's brood expanded rapidly. Soon they were the doting parents of three daughters and a son: Linah, Mariah, Soph, and Robert. When their fifth child, Harriet, was born around 1820, the Rosses gave the new baby the cradle name—or nickname—of Araminta, or Minty for short, possibly to distinguish her from Rit, whose given name was also Harriet. During the decade following Harriet's birth, Rit and Ben would have at least four and as many as six more children. Family records give contradictory accounts regarding the number and names of Harriet's younger siblings.

A Childhood Cut Short

The details of Harriet's early life along Maryland's Eastern Shore are blurry, but historians are sure that her childhood would have been all too fleeting. "Slave children had every stage of childhood cut short, from nursing onward," observes historian Catherine Clinton. "They were propelled into adulthood by slaveholders' impatience."[1]

In common with female children in countless other slave families in the antebellum South, Harriet was put to work at a very tender age caring for her younger siblings. While her parents toiled twelve to fourteen hours a day, six days a week for their owners, little Harriet was left in the sole charge of her two younger brothers, one of whom was still an infant. "When I was four or five years old, my mother cooked up to the big house and left me to take care of the baby and my little brother," Tubman would recall years later. "It was late nights before my mother got home, and when he'd [the baby] get worrying I'd cut a fat chunk of pork and toast it on the coals and put it in his mouth."[2] One night the infant dozed off with the makeshift pacifier hanging out of his mouth. When Rit came home and spied the sleeping infant, for a horrible moment she thought that Harriet had been trying to feed the baby meat and he had choked to death.

Clearly, the struggle to fulfill their duties both to the families they loved and the masters and mistresses they feared took an enormous toll on slave parents like Rit Ross. Life became even more difficult for Rit, Ben, and their brood a few years later when Harriet was about six or seven years old. Once again, the absence of any say in their own fate or that of their children underscored the Rosses' status as mere property. After Mary Brodess Thompson had died unexpectedly in 1810, Rit and the children had continued to reside on the Thompson estate with Ben Ross. Yet, the death of Rit's mistress had left the Rosses deeply uneasy about their own futures. Legally, Harriet's parents belonged to two different owners. Ben belonged to Anthony Thompson, whereas his wife—and their children—belonged to Edward Brodess, Mary's son by her first husband. Rit and Ben realized that once Edward came of age and could legally claim his late mother's property, including her slaves and the Brodess plantation near the village of Bucktown, their family would almost certainly be torn apart. It appeared that the Rosses' worst fears were about to be realized when, shortly after celebrating his twenty-first birthday in 1822, Edward began making arrangements to have an elegant new house constructed on the Brodess property. By 1827, Edward, now married, had settled into his new home and started a family of his own. It was probably around this time, believes Tubman biographer Kate Clifford Larson, that Rit and her children were forced to move to Brodess's farm just outside Bucktown, a 10-mile trek (16km) from the Thompson estate and Ben Ross.

The Rosses' once stable family life would be forever altered when Rit and her brood departed Anthony Thompson's estate. Never again would they all reside together under one roof. The family's new living arrangements did not mean the end of Rit and Ben's more than two-decade-long-marriage, however. The devoted couple reconciled themselves to having an abroad marriage, as unions between slaves who lived on different plantations were popularly known in the antebellum South. In abroad marriages, husbands and wives were typically permitted to visit one another anywhere from once a month to once a week, depending on the distance between their residences and the whims of their masters.

A slave couple often had to settle for an "abroad marriage," in which the husband and wife could see each other only periodically.

Hired Out

When Harriet was forced to abandon Thompson's plantation for the Brodess farm, she knew that her father would no longer be a part of her day-to-day life. What she could not have realized, however, was that she would soon be separated from her mother for long periods of time as well. Most historians agree that Harriet was probably no more than six or seven years of age when she moved to her new home near Bucktown. Yet according to the customs of the antebellum South, she was already considered old enough to be hired out to other masters, and Edward Brodess had every intention of taking advantage of that fact.

During the first half of the nineteenth century, renting out excess slave labor to temporary masters—usually neighbors or relatives—for a few weeks, months, or even years at a time was a common practice among slaveholders in Maryland and throughout much of the upper South. The widespread popularity of the hiring-out system was rooted in the significant economic benefits that the scheme brought to slave owners and slave renters alike. Hiring out "provided valuable income to slaveholders who could not profitably use all of their slaves," explains Kate Clifford Larson, "and it provided a ready labor force to nonslaveholders and other slaveholders who could not, or did not want, to own more slaves."[3]

Whereas white Southerners wholeheartedly embraced the hiring-out system, most of the enslaved workers themselves were considerably less enthusiastic about the practice. Some slaves— particularly unmarried adult males—welcomed the opportunity to travel to other plantations or towns. But for the majority of slaves, the renting-out system only served to compound their misery by fostering long and painful separations among family members. Because children were the single group of slaves most likely to be hired away by their owners, more often than not these

In this illustration of a scene from the antislavery novel *Uncle Tom's Cabin*, a slave mother is forcibly separated from her child. Under slavery, such separations were common.

agonizing separations involved parents and their young sons and daughters. Many slaveholders—including Harriet's new owner, Edward Brodess—seem to have viewed their youngest slaves as little more than nuisances, annoying distractions for their more competent and productive mothers and fathers. Indeed, Brodess was so anxious to get rid of the surplus slave children on his plantation that he frequently rented out the services of Harriet and his other young slaves in exchange for their clothing and board alone.

"Like a Neglected Weed"

Shortly after arriving at the Brodess plantation, little Harriet was sent off to work for her first temporary master, a neighbor of the Brodesses named James Cook. Cook was a farmer and part-time trapper, and his wife was a weaver. Both Cooks were short-tempered and impatient with Harriet, and most nights the homesick girl wept herself to sleep. "I used to sleep on the floor in front of the fireplace . . . and cry and cry," Tubman still remembered vividly decades later. "I used to think all the time if I could only get home and get in my mother's bed, and the funny part of that was, she never had a bed in her life. Nothing but a board box nailed up against the wall and straw laid on it."[4]

One of Harriet's numerous tasks was to check her master's muskrat traps, which Cook set in several nearby marshes and streams. It was an especially onerous job for a small child. In order to retrieve the animals from the traps, Harriet often had to wade in frigid water up to her waist. Predictably, she soon fell ill. Cook and his wife were utterly unsympathetic, accusing Harriet of feigning sickness to get out of doing her chores. Although the little girl exhibited all the symptoms of measles—often a fatal disease during the nineteenth century—she was sent back into the bone-chilling water day after day to inspect the traplines. Finally, to the exasperation of her renters, the disease-weakened child collapsed completely and had to be sent back home to the Brodess plantation and her mother.

Harriet recovered quickly under Rit's loving care. But no sooner had Rit nursed her daughter back to health than Brodess announced that he had found a new renter for Harriet's labor. Harriet was brokenhearted at the prospect of being torn from her mother again. Yet she never questioned that she must do her master's bidding. "I grew up like a neglected weed, ignorant of liberty, having no experience of it,"[5] the adult Tubman bitterly confided to a Northern journalist not long before the start of the Civil War.

The Stinging Lash

Miss Susan, Harriet's new mistress, turned out to be even crueler than the Cooks had been. Susan, a young wife and mother, needed a housecleaner and nursemaid. Married to a farmer of modest means, she was grimly determined to get her money's worth out of Harriet. The little girl toiled from dawn to dusk sweeping, dusting, polishing, and scrubbing. If a job was not done exactly to Miss Susan's specifications, Harriet was whipped severely and ordered to do the work all over again. "When the labors, unremitted for a moment, of the long day were over," wrote Sarah Bradford, Harriet Tubman's friend and first biographer, "there was still no rest for the weary child, for there was a cross baby to be rocked continuously, lest it should wake and disturb the mother's rest."[6] Susan, who slept next to the baby's cradle, always kept a rawhide strap on a shelf just above her bed. If Harriet nodded off and the infant started to wail, down would come the stinging lash upon the exhausted little girl's head and neck. "That poor neck is even now covered with scars which sixty years of life have not been able to efface [erase],"[7] observed Bradford.

One Friday morning as she was clearing the breakfast table, Harriet did something that made her mistress angrier than the young slave had ever seen her before. When Miss Susan's back was turned, she sneaked a small lump of sugar from the sugar bowl. "I never had nothing good; no sweet, no sugar, and that sugar, right by me, did look so nice," Tubman explained to an interviewer years later. To Harriet's dismay, Miss Susan turned around just as she was about to pop the stolen treat into her mouth. Her face contorted with rage, Susan grabbed her whip off the mantelpiece. Impulsively, Harriet decided to make a run for it. "I just flew, and they didn't catch me. I run, and I run, and I run; I passed many a house, but I didn't dare to stop, for they all knew my Missus and they would send me back," Tubman recalled. Harriet kept on running until she was too exhausted to go any further. Spying a large pigsty, she hoisted

Harriet Outsmarts an Abusive Mistress

In 1863, abolitionist Franklin B. Sanborn published a biographical sketch of Harriet Tubman in the antislavery newspaper the *Boston Commonwealth*. The article was based in part on personal interviews with the already famous Underground Railroad agent. In this excerpt from Sanborn's article, the abolitionist recounts a story that Harriet told him about how she outwitted one of the more brutal mistresses to whom she was hired out as a child:

> When quite young she lived with a very pious mistress; but the slaveholder's religion did not prevent her from whipping the young girl for every slight or fancied fault. [Harriet] found that this was usually a morning exercise; so she prepared for it by putting on all the thick clothes she could procure to protect her skin. She made sufficient outcry, however, to convince her mistress that her blows had full effect; and in the afternoon she would take off her wrappings, and dress as well as she could. When invited into family prayers, she preferred to stay on the landing, and pray for herself; "and I prayed to God," she says "to make me strong and able to fight and that's what I've always prayed for ever since."

Quoted in Charles L. Blockson, *The Underground Railroad: First-Person Narratives of Escapes to Freedom in the North.* Upper Saddle River, NJ: Prentice Hall, 1987.

herself over the fence and hid among the pen's occupants: a sow and nine or ten piglets. "There I stayed from Friday until the next Tuesday," Tubman remembered, "fighting with those little pigs for the potato peelings and other scraps that came down in the trough. The old sow would push me away when I tried to get her children's food, and I was awful afraid of her."[8] At last, nearly overcome by hunger and thirst, Harriet concluded that she had no choice but to go back to her brutal mistress and the inevitable flogging.

Slaves were frequently subjected to cruel beatings at the hands of their masters.

Rebellions Small and Great

Despite the brutal punishment she received from Miss Susan's husband for daring to run away, Harriet continued to display a rebellious streak after returning to her owner. During the early 1830s, when Harriet was about eleven or twelve years old, Brodess hired out Rit Ross to cook and clean for his neighbor, a less prosperous farmer by the name of Polish Mills. Harriet knew that she was strictly forbidden to leave Brodess's property. Nonetheless, Harriet obstinately refused to be deprived of her mother's company for a period of weeks or even months when the whole time Rit was living and working just a short walk away from home. Determined to see her beloved parent regardless of the consequences, several nights a week Harriet would slip away from the Brodess plantation and make her way through the dark to the neighbor's farm and her mother. Decades later Harriet Tubman recalled how one of her brothers aided and abetted her in her forbidden nighttime journeys. While Harriet was sneaking out of the slave quarters, he would stand guard by the door of the Rosses' tiny, windowless cabin. There he would scrutinize the nearby roads and woods in case the master, or even more terrifying, a slave patrol, should suddenly materialize out of the darkness.

Armed and mounted patrols for monitoring the movements of slaves had existed in Maryland since the early 1700s. Typically, every adult white male in a community—slaveholder and non-slaveholder alike—was required by law to take a turn riding in the paramilitary patrols. During the early 1830s, when Harriet was making her furtive nighttime visits to her mother at Polish Mills's farm, slave patrols had become more active than ever before in Maryland and throughout the South. Though they overwhelmingly outnumbered blacks and controlled the law, the guns, and the ammunition, Southern whites were running scared during the decades before the Civil War. Fearful that a slave insurrection could erupt at any time, local governments ordered the creation of larger and better-armed slave patrols and strengthened already existing restrictions on black movements. Slaves who ventured off of their master's property unaccompanied by a white—especially after dusk—risked being stopped and interrogated by the whip- and gun-toting patrollers. If slaves could not produce a dated travel pass bearing their master's or mistress's signature, patrollers (called paddyrollers by slaves) had the legal right to whip and beat them severely before they hauled them back to their owners.

The strengthening of slave patrols and constraints on black travel that took place during Harriet's late childhood had its roots in the first and, as it turned out, only sustained slave revolt in U.S. history. Known as Nat Turner's Rebellion, the revolt was named after its leader. Turner was a highly intelligent and charismatic thirty-year-old slave who resided across the Chesapeake Bay from the Ross family in Virginia's Tidewater region. The rebellion, which involved perhaps seventy blacks, broke out in the summer of 1831 in Turner's rural home county of Southampton. Local militiamen and volunteers quickly suppressed the insurrection, but not before the rebels had managed to slaughter almost five dozen white men, women, and children and strike terror in the hearts of Southern whites everywhere. In the wake of Turner's bloody uprising, Harriet and her fellow slaves did not merely face new restrictions on their movements. Throughout the South, state legislatures passed a series of harsh new laws strictly barring slaves from learning to read or write, hold religious services of their own, or gather in groups for any reason whatsoever.

"We Were Always Uneasy"

After Nat Turner's Rebellion, expanded slave patrols and stricter slave codes made day-to-day existence more difficult than ever for the South's 2 million enslaved blacks. Yet for most slaves during the decades leading up to the Civil War, particularly if they resided in the upper South as Harriet and her family did, these hardships paled in comparison with the specter of the auction block.

For slaves in the upper South and especially in the tobacco growing states of Maryland and Virginia, the possibility that they or their loved ones might end up on the auction block increased markedly during the first half of the nineteenth century. During the 1700s, big tobacco plantations dominated much of Virginia and Maryland, including the Eastern Shore where the Ross family lived. But the tobacco plant has a major drawback as an agricultural crop—it rapidly drains the soil of essential nutrients. By the early 1800s, therefore, growing numbers of plantation owners in the upper South were abandoning tobacco cultivation in favor of

Nat Turner and His Rebellion

The leader of the most famous slave insurrection in U.S. history was the son of an African-born mother who despised enslavement and a father who had escaped to freedom in the North. Unlike the vast majority of slaves in the antebellum South, Nat Turner was literate, having been taught to read the Bible at an early age by one of his master's sons. A gifted public speaker, the deeply religious young slave soon became a popular lay preacher in the rural eastern Virginia community where he resided with his master and his family.

When he was in his late twenties, Turner became convinced that God had chosen him to deliver his fellow blacks from bondage. For years he dreamed of inciting a slave revolt. On August 22, 1831, Turner decided the time to act had arrived. Assisted by fewer than a dozen followers, early that morning Turner murdered his owner and his entire family as they slept. Armed with axes and guns, the insurgents then roamed from one plantation to another, recruiting followers and murdering every white man, woman, and child they encountered along the way. Soon the little band of rebels had grown to include about seventy slaves and a handful of free blacks. By August 24, when a force of several hundred militiamen finally quelled the revolt, Turner and his men had slain at least fifty-five whites. The following November, Turner, who had managed to hide out in the woods for six weeks before being tracked down and arrested, was publicly executed. In the hysteria that followed the rebellion, as many as two hundred slaves and freedmen in Virginia were lynched by white mobs.

Nat Turner led the most famous slave uprising in American history. This illustration depicts his capture.

raising wheat, corn, rye, and other grains. This shift from a primarily tobacco-based economy to a predominantly grain-based one had important consequences for the region's slaves. Although a year-round workforce was essential for successful tobacco agriculture, it was not required for the production of cyclical crops such as wheat and corn. As a result, more and more plantation owners opted to sell off their excess slaves after making the switch from tobacco to less labor-intensive grain agriculture.

During the decades leading up to the Civil War, planters in the upper South who wanted to rid themselves of their surplus labor

Large tobacco plantations like this one were common in Maryland in the 1700s.

found a ready market for their slaves in the expanding sugar, rice, and cotton plantations of the lower or Deep South—Georgia, Alabama, Mississippi, Louisiana, South Carolina, and Florida. The explosive growth of cotton agriculture in the lower South was an especially critical factor in that region's voracious demand for slave labor during the first half of the 1800s. The rise of "King Cotton" was directly related to the invention of a simple yet remarkably efficient machine called the cotton gin (short for engine) at the end of the eighteenth century. By quickly removing the plant's numerous seeds from the fluffy cotton fiber, Eli Whitney's famous invention allowed cotton crops to be processed much more rapidly and inexpensively than had ever been possible by hand. Cotton growing became considerably more profitable for Southern farmers, and giant cotton plantations sprang up throughout much of the Deep South. Obtaining the huge numbers of slaves required to plant, care for, and harvest their ever-expanding crop proved challenging for cotton growers, however.

In 1808, Congress had outlawed the importation of African or other foreign slaves into the country, meaning that domestic markets were now the one and only source for the hundreds of thousands of slaves needed to cultivate the vast cotton fields. Slave traders naturally looked to the upper South with its shrinking labor demands for the field hands that their cotton-growing clients further south so desperately desired.

When Harriet was in her late childhood or early adolescence, the Rosses were directly impacted by the burgeoning slave trade between the upper and lower regions of the South. Sometime during the 1830s—the exact year is unknown—Edward Brodess turned over Harriet's older siblings Soph and Linah to Georgia slave traders for several hundred dollars apiece. He appears to have used the money he made from selling the sisters south to purchase additional acreage for his wheat and corn plantation. As far as Brodess was concerned, selling Soph and Linah was no more than a smart business transaction. But the Ross family was shattered by the loss of the two young women, and no one was more affected by the tragedy than Harriet. The image of Soph and Linah "weeping and lamenting"[11] as they were herded off, shackled together with other slaves, would forever haunt her. For many years after her sisters' disappearance, as Tubman told her friend

The invention of the cotton gin, which removed seeds from cotton fiber, helped make cotton a dominant crop in the South.

Sarah Bradford, "she never closed her eyes that she did not imagine she saw the horsemen coming, and heard the screams of women and children, as they were being dragged away to a far worse slavery than that they were enduring there."[12] In the wake of Brodess's heartless act, the chilling realization that he could at any moment decide to fracture her family once again preyed on Harriet's mind constantly. "Every time I saw a white man," Tubman mused, "I was afraid of being carried away."[13] The Ross family had been forced to endure one of the most universally dreaded experience of North American slavery, and they would never be the same again. After Soph and Linah left, Tubman confided to the abolitionist writer Benjamin Drew some two decades later, "We were always uneasy."[14]

Chapter Two

"Liberty, Or Death"

The sale of her older sisters Linah and Soph had a devastating impact on Harriet. More keenly than ever before, she felt the injustice and cruelty of the South's peculiar institution. "Slavery," Tubman declared, "is the next thing to hell. If a person would send another into bondage, he would, it appears to me, be bad enough to send him into hell, if he could."[15] A decade or so after her sisters' disappearance, Harriet was faced with the likelihood that she herself was headed for the auction block. She finally resolved to take control over her own life. With the help of a secret network of courageous black and white volunteers popularly known as the Underground Railroad, Harriet Tubman set off on a dangerous quest to secure her freedom.

"They Carried Me to the House All Bleeding and Fainting"

During the mid-1830s, while Harriet struggled to cope with the crushing loss of her sisters, she still had to endure the day-to-day uncertainties of life as the chattel of Edward Brodess. Throughout Harriet's adolescence, Brodess hired out the young slave to one temporary master after another along the Eastern Shore. Indeed, as a teenager Harriet would spend

Many slaves were forced to perform backbreaking work in the cotton fields.

considerably more time away from the Brodess plantation than she would on it.

Most of Harriet's renters during this period were small farmers who needed some extra help in their fields, especially during the hectic planting and harvesting seasons. By the age of thirteen or so, Harriet had almost completely abandoned housework for field-work. Although hoeing and harvesting were more physically demanding jobs than cleaning house or cooking, Harriet welcomed her new status as a field hand. She preferred the relative freedom of toiling out-of-doors in the company of her fellow slaves to being cooped up inside all day under the smothering scrutiny of an exacting mistress such as the ill-tempered Miss Susan.

One autumn when Harriet was still in her early teens, Brodess hired her out to a local farmer to help with harvesting his flax crop. It was during this period that one of the most traumatic events in Harriet Tubman's life took place. One evening after her work in the fields was finished, Harriet's master ordered her to purchase a few items for him at the village dry goods store. Harriet had completed her shopping and was heading toward the door when a slave from a nearby plantation suddenly dashed into the store. At the young man's heels was an extremely angry-looking white overseer. Spotting Harriet, the overseer ordered her to help him tie up the slave so that he could give the runaway a whipping. Daringly, Harriet refused. The overseer then picked up a lead weight from the counter and hurled it at the escapee. The heavy projectile fell short of its mark, however, and struck Harriet a crushing blow on the forehead. Harriet, who had covered her hair with a shawl before going out that night, later recalled how the weight "broke my skull and cut a piece of that shawl clean off and drove it into my head. They carried me to the house all bleeding and fainting. I had no bed, no place to lie down at all, and they laid me on the seat of the loom, and I stayed there all that day and the next."[16]

Although Harriet's wound was obviously severe, no one in the big house, as masters' homes were called, bothered to fetch a physician to examine the young slave. Resolved to get his money's worth out of her, Harriet's renter ordered her back to the fields as soon as she could stand unaided. "I went to work again," she recalled, "and there I worked with the blood and sweat rolling down my face till I couldn't see."[17] Grumbling that the injured girl was not "worth the salt that seasons her grub," the disgruntled farmer finally sent Harriet back to her owner.[18]

Under her mother's care, Harriet slowly regained her strength. Yet she would never completely recover from her terrible head wound. For the rest of her life she would be

Even though it was physically demanding, Harriet preferred working in the fields to cooking and housecleaning.

plagued by abrupt and crippling episodes of extreme fatigue. Some three decades after Harriet's fateful encounter with the overseer, journalist Franklin Sanborn observed: "The blow produced a disease of the brain which . . . still makes her very lethargic. She cannot remain quiet fifteen minutes without appearing to fall asleep. It is not refreshing slumber; but a heavy, weary condition which exhausts her."[19]

New Opportunities

Despite her periodic episodes of overwhelming drowsiness, by her late teens Harriet had developed into a highly competent and productive worker. Although she was barely 5 feet tall (1.5m), she possessed a muscular build and remarkable stamina and excelled at plowing, clearing timber, and other especially strenuous tasks usually reserved for male slaves. Yet because Harriet was female, her time could be rented out at a lower rate than that of a bondman. Consequently, she was highly sought after as a temporary laborer by the farmers and timber harvesters of Dorchester County. Possibly in recognition of her hard work, during the late 1830s Brodess did something uncharacteristically generous: He permitted Harriet to hire her own time out as she pleased after she had paid him a set yearly fee of about fifty dollars. Harriet's work-for-hire arrangement allowed her to enjoy a small measure of independence while at the same time giving her the chance to earn some money of her own. So industrious was Harriet that she was able to make enough extra cash in one year to purchase a pair of oxen.

In about 1837 or 1838, Brodess allowed Harriet to hire herself out to John Stewart, the owner of a flourishing lumber business located near Tobacco Stick and the Thompson estate, where her father still resided. To Harriet's delight, Stewart employed her father, Ben Ross, as a timber foreman whenever the Thompson family could spare him from their lumbering operation. Over the course of the five to six years that she spent with Stewart, Harriet often found herself working under her father's direct supervision, cutting logs and hauling lumber to be transported to shipyards in Dorchester County or the bustling port of Baltimore.

Laboring for John Stewart provided Harriet with the opportunity to renew her relationship with her father. It also brought her into a wider community of slaves and free blacks who toiled as

In 1963, actress Ruby Dee, shown here with costar Ossie Davis as John Tubman, portrayed Harriet Tubman in "Go Down, Moses," an episode of the CBS historical series "The Great Adventure."

timbermen, field hands, and boatmen in the economically vibrant northwestern corner of Dorchester County. Among the numerous African Americans, enslaved and free, with whom Harriet became acquainted during her years in the Tobacco Stick area, one was destined to play a significant role in her life.

John Tubman, Freedman

In 1844, when Harriet would have been in her early twenties, she wed John Tubman, a free black. Little is known about Harriet's first spouse, except that he was born to free parents in northern Dorchester County about 1815. Like other freedmen in the Tobacco Stick area, he probably eked out a modest living as a field hand or timberman, laboring for a few weeks or months at a time for a number of temporary employers.

John Tubman was part of a growing population of free blacks who lived and worked in Maryland during the mid-nineteenth century. During the decades leading up to the Civil War, the number of free African Americans in the South, and particularly in border states such as Maryland, expanded steadily. The vast

In this illustration, a slave mother grieves after being separated from her child. Tubman's family was similarly broken up when she was very young.

majority of them had either been manumitted (set free) by their masters or were the children or grandchildren of freed slaves. A small number had managed to scrape together enough money to buy their freedom from their owners or had had their freedom purchased for them by others. As Maryland's free black population multiplied, marriages between free and enslaved African Americans increased as well. Many slaveholders, however, fearful that any fraternization between the two black communities would lead to discontent and even rebellion among their slaves, forbade such couplings, and free-slave marriages remained relatively rare in the state throughout the antebellum period.

According to family lore, Harriet was deeply in love with her freedman husband. In light of the considerable sacrifices he had to make to wed Harriet, it seems likely that John was also in love at the time of his marriage. According to the laws of Maryland and every other slaveholding state, children born to black women automatically inherited their mother's status as free or enslaved. This meant that John possessed no legal rights to any of the offspring he and Harriet might have together. His children, like his wife, would be the property of Harriet's owner, Edward Brodess, to dispose of as he saw fit. Because a slave's master could choose to disregard the couple's relationship, any union between a slave and a free black—as between a bondman and a bondwoman— was not a legally binding contract but merely an informal arrangement. Thus, even though Brodess had given his consent to Harriet's union with a freedman, if he suddenly decided to sell Harriet to another owner who disapproved of such marriages, John Tubman's entire personal life could be thrown into limbo.

Harriet Tubman Makes a Disturbing Discovery

A year after marrying John Tubman, Harriet did something quite unusual for a slave: She hired a lawyer. For years she had heard rumors that her mother was being held in bondage illegally. Perhaps spurred on by her recent marriage to a free man, Harriet Tubman finally decided to find out once and for all if there was any truth to the stories. In 1845, she paid a lawyer five dollars of her hard-earned savings to locate and review the will of Rit's original owner, Athon Pattison, the grandfather of Mary Brodess Thompson and great-grandfather of Edward Brodess.

When, after much searching, the lawyer finally unearthed the decades-old will, Tubman became convinced that a grave miscarriage of justice had occurred. Although the document's wording was vague, the will seemed to indicate that Pattison wished Rit to be freed when she reached the age of forty-five and any children she might eventually have to be emancipated when they reached the same age. Rit's birth date had never been officially recorded, but Tubman was sure that her mother was well past fifty. Edward Brodess, she concluded, had deliberately violated the terms of his great-grandfather's will and cheated her mother out of her freedom. Moreover, because Maryland law stipulated that only slaves for life could be sold out of state and Linah and Soph, like all of Rit's children, were supposed to be freed when they turned forty-five, Tubman was convinced that Brodess had illegally sold her sisters south a decade earlier.

The discovery of Athon Pattison's will had a profound effect on Tubman. She was enraged by what she believed to be Edward Brodess's deceit. Yet she felt powerless to help her mother or her older sisters. An illiterate slave such as herself could never hope to prevail in a court of law against a prominent white landowner like Brodess, or for that matter against any white person, she realized. Tubman was becoming more and more convinced that there was only one way out of the hell that was slavery, both for herself and her loved ones. No matter how daunting the prospect of such a perilous and unknown undertaking might be, they must set aside their fears and take the long journey north to freedom.

Dreaming of Freedom

Over the next several years, Harriet Tubman became more and more preoccupied with the idea of fleeing the Eastern Shore for the free states that she had heard lay just to the north of Maryland. During bouts of extreme drowsiness, Tubman had vivid daydreams, powerful visions that she believed came directly from God. After her distressing consultation with the lawyer regarding Athon Pattison's will, Tubman was haunted by the same vision over and over again. In the dream she was flying northward, soaring like a bird over forests and rivers, farm fields and towns. Suddenly she found her way blocked by a tall fence. She knew that freedom lay just on the other side of the high barrier but feared she lacked the strength to fly over it. Just

Harriet Jacobs: Incidents in the Life of a Slave Girl

One of the most candid and widely read memoirs of slave life in American history was penned by a former bondwoman from North Carolina named Harriet Jacobs. Published in 1861, Jacobs's *Incidents in the Life of a Slave Girl* recounted the great lengths to which the young wife and mother was willing to go to escape from her sexually abusive master, Dr. James Norcom. Before fleeing at last to the free state of New York, Jacobs spent nearly a decade hiding in the dark attic of a tiny shed attached to a relative's house. In this selection from *Incidents in the Life of a Slave Girl*, Jacobs vividly describes the appalling conditions under which she was forced to live for seven long years:

> The garret was only nine feet long and seven wide. The highest part was three feet high, and sloped down abruptly to the loose board floor. There was no admission for either light or air. . . . The air was stifling: the darkness was total. A bed had been spread on the floor. I could sleep quite comfortably on one side; but the slope was so sudden that I could not turn on the other side without hitting the roof. The rats and mice ran over my bed. . . . In my small den day and night were all the same. . . . This continued darkness was oppressive. It seemed horrible to sit or lie in a cramped position day after day, without one gleam of light. Yet I would have chosen this, rather than my lot as a slave.

Quoted in Karin Coddon, ed., *Runaway Slaves*. San Diego: Greenhaven, 2004, p. 69.

as she was about to give up and turn back, however, a group of white-robed ladies would beckon to her from the other side of the fence. When Tubman flew closer, the women would reach out their hands to her and gently pull her over the lofty barrier.

In her daydreams Tubman always managed to get to the other side of the fence—and the freedom she so longed for. Yet in her more lucid moments she could not help but worry about the terrible risks all runaways faced. Attempting to escape slavery was a felony crime in the antebellum South, and if caught, a runaway slave could expect to be whipped severely, branded on the forehead or hands with a hot iron, or mutilated, usually by having his or her ears cut off. Generous rewards were offered for the return of runaways, and killing a fugitive slave who resisted arrest was not considered a crime under Maryland law or the laws of any other slaveholding state. Little wonder that Tubman kept on delaying her escape year after year, even though the dream of freedom was never far from her mind.

Then, late in the winter of 1849, an event occurred that played a critical role in convincing Tubman finally to turn her dream of self-liberation into reality, regardless of the possible dangers. On March 9, 1849, the man who had been Tubman's master for almost her entire life passed away. For the first time she began to consider the idea that remaining in bondage might actually be the more risky course of action than attempting to escape it.

The Death of Edward Brodess

At the time of Edward Brodess's death in March 1849, Harriet Tubman was working for her owner's stepbrother, Dr. Anthony C. Thompson, most likely at his main residence near the Choptank River, about 15 miles (24km) northeast of Tobacco Stick. It appears that Brodess had also hired out Harriet's younger brothers Henry and Benjamin Ross to Thompson to labor on the doctor's rambling riverside estate.

Soon after Brodess's death, Tubman began hearing rumors that her late master had left his widow Eliza deeply in debt. In order to meet her pressing financial obligations, Eliza Brodess intended to sell several of the family's slaves south. At first Tubman did not take the rumors seriously. Then, late in the summer of 1849, a slave on a neighboring plantation who had contacts in the Bucktown area approached Tubman with disturbing news. Eliza, the man told her, had been talking about selling Tubman—and possibly Benjamin and Henry as well—to a Georgia slave trader who was promising to pay planters in the Bucktown area top dollar for young, healthy field hands.

Some ten years earlier, Tubman had witnessed her shackled older siblings herded away in a slave coffle, bound for the vast plantations of the lower South. Tubman was filled with dread at the thought of following in her sisters' footsteps, neither of whom had ever been heard from again. Terrifying stories about life downriver had circulated through the slave quarters of every plantation she had ever worked on. Blacks in the Deep South rarely made it to old age, people said, because they were literally used up by the backbreaking labor of picking 200 pounds (90km) or more of cotton a day under a blistering sun. Once she had let herself be dragged into this miserable existence, Tubman reasoned, her chances of escaping it alive were poor. Pennsylvania was at most a ten-day journey on foot from Dorchester County; but reaching Pennsylvania or any other free state from a plantation in the Deep South would entail a grueling trek of many weeks or even months through hostile slaveholding territories and rugged, unfamiliar terrain.

Cold Feet

Harriet Tubman was determined to escape the chains of slavery while she still could. But she did not want to run alone. Tubman's

Slaves, including Tubman's older siblings, were sometimes shackled together in a coffle like the one shown in this engraving.

source had informed her that Benjamin and Henry were also in imminent danger of being sold downriver by Eliza Brodess, and Tubman was determined to talk her brothers into accompanying her on her perilous journey north. Convincing her brothers to go with her proved difficult, however. Both men were terrified of being caught by trigger-happy slave patrols or bounty hunters, and Benjamin, who had a wife and several young children, was reluctant to leave his family. But at last Tubman prevailed, and the threesome began plotting an escape plan.

Although Harriet Tubman tried to convince her husband to travel north with her and her brothers, John Tubman wanted no part of the scheme. Life was far from easy for free people of color

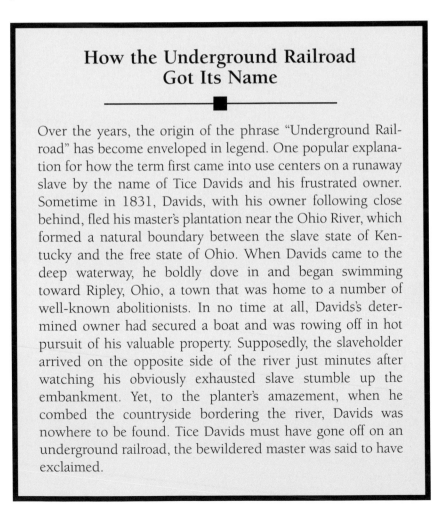

How the Underground Railroad Got Its Name

Over the years, the origin of the phrase "Underground Railroad" has become enveloped in legend. One popular explanation for how the term first came into use centers on a runaway slave by the name of Tice Davids and his frustrated owner. Sometime in 1831, Davids, with his owner following close behind, fled his master's plantation near the Ohio River, which formed a natural boundary between the slave state of Kentucky and the free state of Ohio. When Davids came to the deep waterway, he boldly dove in and began swimming toward Ripley, Ohio, a town that was home to a number of well-known abolitionists. In no time at all, Davids's determined owner had secured a boat and was rowing off in hot pursuit of his valuable property. Supposedly, the slaveholder arrived on the opposite side of the river just minutes after watching his obviously exhausted slave stumble up the embankment. Yet, to the planter's amazement, when he combed the countryside bordering the river, Davids was nowhere to be found. Tice Davids must have gone off on an underground railroad, the bewildered master was said to have exclaimed.

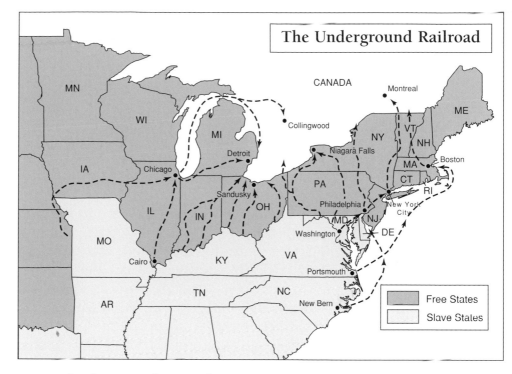

The Underground Railroad

CANADA

Montreal

Collingwood

ME

MN

WI

MI

VT

NY

NH

Detroit

Niagara Falls

MA

Boston

IA

Chicago

CT

RI

Sandusky

PA

New York City

IL

IN

OH

Philadelphia

MO

MD

NJ

DE

Washington

Cairo

KY

VA

Portsmouth

AR

TN

NC

New Bern

Free States
Slave States

in Maryland or anywhere in the South during the decades before the Civil War. State laws preventing free blacks from assembling for any reason severely restricted the ability of African Americans to establish their own schools, mutual aid societies, or churches. Yet at the same time, free blacks were barred from virtually all white organizations in the South, religious and secular. Nevertheless, John Tubman clearly preferred to remain in the only home he had ever known rather than commit himself to a new life in a strange land among people who might turn out to be even more hostile toward free blacks than his white neighbors in Maryland were.

According to some accounts, Harriet Tubman did not inform her husband of the exact time or date of her departure, lest he try to prevent her from taking part in such a hazardous—and in his view—ill-judged scheme. With or without John Tubman's knowledge, one clear night toward the end of September, Harriet Tubman, Benjamin, and Henry set off on their long journey north, depending on nothing more than the North Star and their own instincts to guide them. By daybreak, terrified of losing their way—and even more so of recapture—Tubman's brothers had refused to continue. Although Tubman pleaded with them to reconsider, the two men were determined to return to Thompson's plantation before their absence had been noticed. When Tubman stubbornly refused even to consider turning back, Benjamin and Henry lost all patience with their older sister and literally "dragged her back with them,"[20] according to Sarah Bradford.

With the threat of being sold south still hanging over her head, Tubman was not about to give up so easily on her quest for freedom, however. If her brothers would not accompany her north then she would just have to go by herself, she resolved. Years later, Tubman explained to Sarah Bradford how she had arrived at her bold decision to make the treacherous journey alone: "I had reasoned this out in my mind; there was one of two things I had a *right* to, liberty, or death; if I could not have one, I would have the other; for no man should take me alive; I should fight for my liberty as long as my strength lasted, and when the time came for me to go, the Lord would let them take me."[21]

Only a few nights after she and her brothers had embarked on their ill-fated trek north, Harriet Tubman slipped out of the tiny slave cabin she shared with her husband once again. But this time around she intended to do things differently. As soon as she had made it safely off Thompson's property, Tubman did not immediately head in the direction of the North Star as she, Henry, and Benjamin had done. Instead, she made her way through the darkness to the house of one of her master's neighbors, a white woman. Her failed escape attempt had taught her one thing, notes historian Fergus Bordewich: "that the odds against escaping without help were close to insurmountable. She would not make the same mistake again."[22]

According to one account, when Tubman arrived at the house of the unnamed neighbor, she presented the woman with a patchwork quilt, a treasured belonging that she dared not give to any of her enslaved friends or relatives for fear they would be accused of knowing about her escape plans. In turn the woman presented Tubman with a slip of paper on which two names had been written and directed her to the home of the first individual, who, she assured Tubman, would then direct her to the residence of the second. Harriet Tubman had just had her first encounter with the secret organization that would someday make her one of the best-known and most admired African Americans in U.S. history: the Underground Railroad.

The Underground Railroad

The term "Underground Railroad" first appeared during the early 1830s, shortly after steam-powered trains were introduced to America from England. Loosely organized networks to help slaves escape to freedom had existed in the United States since the final decades of the previous century, however. During the years following the Revolutionary War, countless runaways were assisted in their bids for freedom by free blacks and some whites, the vast majority of them Northerners. By then slavery was rapidly disappearing throughout the northern half of the United States, chiefly for economic reasons but also because of a growing conviction among many white Northerners—particularly Quakers, Unitarians, Jews, and members of other religious groups—that slavery was a deeply immoral and unjust system.

From about 1830 on, the abolitionist movement to outlaw slavery in the United States strengthened significantly in the North, where New Jersey had become the last state to abolish the institution in 1804. Spurred on by the North's increasing anti-slavery sentiment, organized efforts to help guide fugitive slaves to the free states and Canada also expanded. As the phrase "Underground Railroad" came into general use during the 1830s, the network's growing numbers of volunteers began adopting popular railroad terms to describe themselves and their secret work. For example, private homes and businesses where runaways were hidden along their way north were called stations and their owners dubbed stationmasters; the men and women who escorted fugitives to freedom were called conductors; and the escaped slaves themselves were variously referred to as passengers, cargo, or packages.

It seems likely that Harriet Tubman first became familiar with the Underground Railroad while working for lumber merchant John Stewart in the Tobacco Stick area during the late 1830s and early 1840s. Laboring for Stewart allowed her to mingle with a much wider community of free blacks than she ever had before. Many of her new acquaintances, and especially the black mariners whose ships transported Stewart's timber to Baltimore

Samuel D. Burris,
Prominent African American Conductor on
Delaware's Underground Railroad

Some historians have suggested that Harriet Tubman sought shelter with the Underground Railroad operative William Brinkley in Camden, Delaware, on her way to Pennsylvania in 1849. If she did not, at the very least during her stay in Camden she would have heard about another prominent African American conductor who had only recently been forced to flee town because of his antislavery activities, Samuel D. Burris.

Little is known about Burris's early years except that he was born to free parents in Kent County, Delaware, in 1808. By the mid-1840s, Burris had moved to Camden and become active in the Underground Railroad, assisting slaves to escape from his home state to freedom in Pennsylvania. Burris's undercover activities placed him in grave danger: In the state of Delaware, a free black convicted of helping a runaway could be sold into slavery. During the summer of 1847, Burris was caught in the act of leading an escaped Delaware slave named Maria Mathews toward the Pennsylvania border. After spending more than a year in jail awaiting trial, Burris was finally convicted of aiding a runaway and sentenced to spend the next seven years of his life in slavery.

Unbeknownst to Burris, however, his many friends in the Pennsylvania Anti-Slavery Society had formulated a plan for freeing him. When Samuel was put on the auction block, a member of the Anti-Slavery Society, posing as a slave trader, outbid all of Burris's other potential buyers. Burris's friend then smuggled the Underground Railroad conductor and his wife and children to Philadelphia, where the family lived quietly for several years before moving to California. Burris died in San Francisco in 1869, just four years after the end of the Civil War.

and other ports, were undoubtedly well informed about the secret linkages of people that helped runaways escape the Eastern Shore for Pennsylvania and other Northern destinations. When Tubman set out on her second escape attempt in the fall of 1849, the name of the white female neighbor whose help she sought may well have come to her from one of her free acquaintances in the Tobacco Stick area.

Little is known about Harriet Tubman's trek to freedom in late 1849. She never provided a clear account regarding the details of her route and the helpers who gave her directions or shelter along her way northward. Some scholars have speculated that Tubman first traveled northeast toward Camden, Delaware, where she may have stayed with William Brinkley, a free black and prominent local Underground Railroad agent, then north through Wilmington to Pennsylvania, a journey of about 90 miles (145km). When, after seven or eight days on the road, she reached the Pennsylvania border, Harriet Tubman finally got her first taste of freedom after nearly thirty years in bondage.

Chapter Three

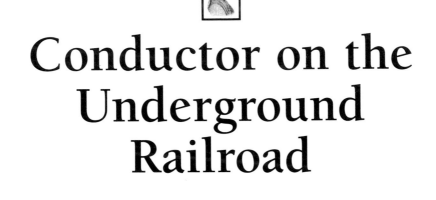

Conductor on the Underground Railroad

During the late 1840s, when Harriet Tubman escaped to Pennsylvania, an estimated one thousand slaves were fleeing to freedom each year in the United States, the majority of them from border states such as Maryland, Virginia, and Delaware. Most ran spontaneously and without assistance, traveling under the cover of darkness along back roads or through woods, swamps, and fields with only the North Star to direct them. But like Harriet Tubman, many others turned to the men and women of the Underground Railroad for guidance and shelter on their long and perilous journey north. Barely a year after escaping slavery, Tubman herself became a vital link in the Underground Railroad. Yet even in an organization whose members were famous for their dedication and courage, Tubman's extraordinary spirit of self-sacrifice and sheer grit set her apart. By the mid-1850s, Tubman's willingness repeatedly to jeopardize her hard-won liberty—and her very life—to help others find freedom had made her one of the Underground Railroad's most effective conductors.

"A Stranger in a Strange Land"

When she first stepped foot in the free state of Pennsylvania, Tubman later mused, she felt as though she had died and gone to paradise. "When I found I had crossed that line," she told Sarah Bradford, "I looked at my hands to see if I was the same person. There was such a glory over everything; the sun came like gold through the trees and fields, and I felt like I was in Heaven."[23]

Yet Tubman's joy quickly gave way to a sense of overwhelming loneliness. In gaining her liberty she had lost her family and the only home she had ever known. "I had crossed the line of which I had so long been dreaming," she reflected. "I was free; but there was no one to welcome me to the land of freedom, I was a stranger in a strange land, and my home after all was down in the . . . [slave] quarters with the old folks and my brothers and sisters." Convinced that her loved ones would never attempt to flee on their own, Tubman resolved to return south and personally conduct them to Pennsylvania, regardless of the tremendous risks to herself. She later told Sarah Bradford: "But to this solemn resolution I came; I was free, and they should be free also; I would make a home for them in the North, and the Lord helping me, I would bring them all here."[24]

Her ambitious rescue scheme was bound to require money, Tubman realized. She quickly decided that the best place to find a job was Philadelphia, Pennsylvania's biggest city

This illustration from about 1850 shows Harriet Tubman around the age of 30.

and home to the largest community of free blacks in North America. In Philadelphia Tubman soon found steady employment as a cook and laundress. Within a year of fleeing north, she had managed to save enough from her meager earnings to fund her first rescue mission: a trip to Baltimore, Maryland, to liberate her niece, Kessiah Bowley, and her two young children, James and Araminta Bowley.

First Rescue Missions

Although family accounts of Kessiah Bowley are sketchy and occasionally contradictory, scholars believe that she was the daughter of Tubman's older sister Linah, who was sold south by Edward Brodess sometime during the 1830s along with Soph Ross. Tubman seems to have been particularly close to Kessiah, who always referred to her aunt as Sister Harriet. Only a few years apart in age, Harriet and Kessiah may have been raised virtually as sisters. Historians speculate that when her own mother was sold away, young Kessiah probably moved in with her grandmother, Harriet Tubman's mother, Rit Ross.

In December 1850, Tubman received a troubling message from free relatives and friends in Baltimore. Eliza Brodess had publicly announced her intention to auction off Kessiah, James, and Araminta at the Dorchester County courthouse in the town of Cambridge, near the Chesapeake Bay. Tubman also learned that Kessiah's husband, John, a free black, had devised a daring scheme to smuggle his family out of Cambridge and ferry them up the Chesapeake to Baltimore in a rowboat or canoe. From Baltimore, Bowley then hoped to find his way north to Pennsylvania.

Determined to shepherd her beloved niece and her family to freedom personally, Tubman rushed to Baltimore. In order to get there as quickly as possible, she may have traveled by train, using forged papers that identified her as a free woman. Shortly after her arrival in Maryland, word came to Tubman that Kessiah, John, and their children had made it safely across the bay. Tubman hastily located a hiding place for the family, perhaps in the Baltimore home of Underground Railroad agent Jacob Gibbs, one of the organization's many free black volunteers. A few days later, Tubman and the Bowleys slipped out of Maryland bound for

On Becoming Free

In his autobiography, the renowned antislavery activist Frederick Douglass struggles to describe his overwhelming joy at finding himself a free man for the first time:

My free life began on the third of September, 1838. On the morning of the 4th of that month, after an anxious and most perilous but safe journey, I found myself in the big city of New York, a *free man*. . . . Though dazzled with the wonders which met me on every hand, my thoughts could not be much withdrawn from my strange situation. For the moment the dreams of my youth, and the hopes of my manhood, were completely fulfilled. The bonds that had held me to "old master" were broken. No man now had the right to call me his slave or assert mastery over me. I was in the rough and tumble of an outdoor world, to take my chance with the rest of its busy number. I have often been asked, how I felt when first I found myself on free soil. . . . A new world had opened upon me. If life is more than breath, and the "quick round of blood," I lived more in one day than in a year of my slave life. It was a time of joyous excitement which words can but tamely describe. In a letter written to a friend soon after reaching New York, I said: "I felt as one might feel upon escape from a den of lions." Anguish and grief, like darkness and rain, may be depicted: but gladness and joy, like the rainbow, defy the skill of pen or pencil.

Abolitionist Frederick Douglass published his autobiography, in which he described his escape from slavery, in 1881.

Frederick Douglass, *The Life and Times of Frederick Douglass, Written by Himself,* 1881. Reprint, New York: Carol, 1995, p. 202.

Only a year after escaping slavery herself, Tubman became a conductor on the Underground Railroad.

Pennsylvania and freedom. Little is known about Tubman's first rescue mission except that she escorted her relatives all the way to her new hometown of Philadelphia. Heartened by her success with the Bowleys, Tubman returned to the Baltimore area a few months after their escape, this time to guide one of her brothers—

probably her youngest sibling, Moses Ross—and two other men who may have been Moses's friends, to free soil.

Going Home to Dorchester County

In the autumn of 1851, Harriet Tubman returned to the county of her birth for the first time since her escape from Dr. Thompson's plantation. Just how Tubman got to Dorchester County is a mystery. She may have followed the same route she took on first departing the Eastern Shore for Pennsylvania, perhaps even staying with the same Underground Railroad stationmasters who had sheltered and fed her two years earlier in Camden, Delaware, and elsewhere along her way.

Yet even with the assistance of her allies in the Underground Railroad, Tubman faced enormous dangers in returning to her old home. In late 1849, Eliza Brodess had posted a reward of several hundred dollars for Tubman's recapture, and since Tubman had worked as a temporary laborer for numerous farmers and timbermen throughout central and western Dorchester County, her face and name were well-known in the area. Nevertheless, Harriet Tubman had her heart set on making the perilous trip home. She missed her husband terribly and was prepared to risk everything in order to bring John Tubman back to Philadelphia with her.

From a safe house somewhere in Dorchester County—perhaps the home of the white woman who had first linked her up with the Underground Railroad two years earlier—Harriet Tubman sent an urgent message to her husband, pleading with him to accompany her to Pennsylvania at once. But just as he had two years earlier, John Tubman again declined to leave Maryland. Through an intermediary, he informed Harriet Tubman that he had taken another wife—a free black like himself this time—and he had no intention of abandoning his new spouse.

Harriet Tubman was furious. She wanted nothing more than to confront her unfaithful husband face-to-face. Years later she confided to a friend that "she did not care what massa did to her, she thought she would go right in and make all the trouble she could, she was determined to see her old man once more." After cooling down a bit, however, Harriet Tubman realized "how foolish it was just for temper to make mischief," concluding "that if [John] could do without her, she could do without him."[25] Not about to waste an opportunity to help others reach freedom, with the assistance of her Underground Railroad contacts Harriet Tubman tracked down several local slaves who were prepared to flee at a moment's notice and escorted them all the way to Philadelphia.

On to Canada

Exhibiting remarkable stamina and nerve, Harriet Tubman made one more trip to the Eastern Shore in 1851, sneaking back into Dorchester County in December to liberate eleven slaves. The large group of runaways included one of her younger brothers— perhaps James Isaac—and probably several other relatives. This time around, Tubman did not terminate her rescue mission in Philadelphia. Instead, she conducted her party through Upstate New York and into the modern-day Canadian province of Ontario, then known as Canada West. Almost certainly, Tubman and her party traveled by rail for most of their long trek through the northern United States, using money donated by Underground Railroad operatives and from Tubman's personal savings to purchase the train tickets. Years later Tubman revealed to historian Wilbur Siebert that when she escorted a group of escapees from Philadelphia to Canada West, she typically "proceeded by steam railroad to New York [City], and from there she took the train to Albany, where [Underground Railroad agent] Stephen Myers looked after her and her charges."[26] From Albany, Tubman and her party would head by rail to Rochester, where the famous black abolitionist Frederick Douglass often put them up in his home for the night before helping them catch one last train, this time for Buffalo, New York, and the suspension bridge over Niagara Falls.

By late 1851, when she made her first trip over Niagara Falls with her younger brother and ten other fugitives in tow, Tubman had come to the conclusion that she could not "trust Uncle Sam with my people any longer," as she later told Sarah Bradford. The chief reason for Tubman's newfound determination to whisk her charges "clear off to Canada,"[27] as she put it, was one of the most controversial pieces of legislation in U.S. history: the Fugitive Slave Law of 1850. Ever since the first Fugitive Slave Act passed Congress in 1793, slave owners or their agents had possessed the right to pursue and seize escaped slaves, even in the free states of the North. The Fugitive Slave Law approved by Congress nearly sixty years later at the urging of its Southern membership had considerably more clout than the original act, however. By making it easier for owners to retrieve their lost property than ever before, the new law put all runaways in free states and territories in immediate peril. Local police and other authorities were now

Frederick Douglass, Underground Railroad Operative

Although Frederick Douglass is best known as an antislavery lecturer and writer, he was also a volunteer in the Underground Railroad, and his home in Rochester, New York, was often used as a safe house by groups of fugitives fleeing north into Canada. In his memoirs, the former slave described a visit to his Rochester home by a party of eleven runaways. Although Douglass never identified the group, most historians believe that it was almost certainly the party of eleven slaves that Harriet Tubman brought from Maryland to Canada in late 1851. From Douglass's account, it appears that he personally raised the funds to pay for the group's railroad tickets from Rochester to Saint Catharines, on the other side of the Canadian border from Buffalo, New York. Douglass wrote:

> On one occasion I had eleven fugitives at the same time under my roof, and it was necessary for them to remain with me until I could collect sufficient money to get them on to Canada. It was the largest number I ever had at any one time, and I had some difficulty in providing so many with food and shelter, but, as may well be imagined, they were not very fastidious in either direction, and were well content with very plain food, and a strip of carpet on the floor for a bed, or a place on the straw in the barn loft.

Frederick Douglass, *The Life and Times of Frederick Douglass, Written by Himself*, 1881. Reprint, New York: Carol, 1995, p. 272.

compelled to cooperate with slave catchers hunting runaways within their jurisdiction. Moreover, the new legislation made it a federal crime for private citizens to hinder the recapture of a fugitive slave in any way. Any individual—Northern or Southern—convicted of aiding or abetting a runaway could receive a huge fine or even jail time.

Lauded by most Southern whites, the Fugitive Slave Law of 1850 caused a major uproar among both whites and blacks in the North. Above the Mason-Dixon Line which separated slave states from free states, even many whites who did not support the immediate abolition of slavery deeply resented the new law, viewing it as an attempt by arrogant Southern slaveholders to make Northerners serve as their personal agents. Within the North's large African American community, the new legislation evoked feelings of terror as well as resentment. Now former slaves could

This illustration fancifully depicts the effects of the Fugitive Slave Law, which made it illegal to assist a runaway slave.

no longer take their safety for granted anywhere in the United States. By the end of 1851, when Harriet Tubman conducted her first group of fugitives to Ontario, thousands of ex-slaves had already abandoned their new homes in Northern cities and towns to start their lives over again in British Canada, where slavery was outlawed and American slaveholders had long been denied extradition for their fugitive "property." The exact number of blacks who fled to the United States' northern neighbor during the decade between the passage of the Fugitive Slave Law and the outbreak of the Civil War is unknown. But historians speculate that at least twenty thousand African Americans crossed into Canada during this period, many of them having found their way to a more secure freedom with the assistance of Underground Railroad agents like Harriet Tubman.

In the winter of 1851, after Tubman had guided her eleven passengers across the Niagara, she deposited the fugitives in Saint Catharines, Ontario, directly across the suspension bridge from Buffalo, New York. Over the next few years, the little town near the U.S.-Canadian border became a kind of home away from home for the Underground Railroad conductor. By 1852, not only Tubman's brother but also her favorite niece, Kessiah Bowley, and her family had settled there. Tubman soon fell into a pattern of spending Christmas and most of the winter months with her relatives in Saint Catharines, then returning to Philadelphia in the spring to seek employment as a cook or laundress. Typically, she would work in Philadelphia or the nearby resort town of Cape May, New Jersey, through the early autumn, putting every cent she could into her travel fund. Then in the late fall or early winter, Tubman would make the hazardous journey into Maryland at least once to rescue family members, friends, and others from the horrors of slavery. More often than not, she escorted her charges all the way to southern Ontario. By the winter of 1853–1854, she had completed at least six rescue operations, conducting dozens of slaves to Pennsylvania, New York, or Canada.

William Still and Thomas Garrett

The success of Tubman's rescue missions depended first and foremost on her own courage, resourcefulness, and dedication. Yet her daring operations also required the concerted efforts of many helpers, black and white, within the Underground Railroad. From the early 1850s on, the two stationmasters with whom she worked most closely were also two of the Underground Railroad's most famous and influential leaders—William Still of Philadelphia and Thomas Garrett of Wilmington, Delaware.

William Still was the youngest of eighteen children. William was born free in New Jersey in 1821, although both his parents had once been enslaved. In 1844, the largely self-taught Still moved to Philadelphia and soon became active in the city's antislavery movement. Three years later, the twenty-six-year-old was hired as a clerk by the Pennsylvania Society for the Abolition of Slavery. By 1852, in recognition of his outstanding organizational skills and tireless devotion to the cause of freedom, Still had been promoted to the position of executive director of the society's General Vigilance Committee, so named because its goal was to be ever vigilant in protecting and assisting fugitives. By the middle of the nineteenth century, virtually every major city in the Northeast had its own vigilance or fugitive aid committee, "but the group in Philadelphia had no equal, in large part because of Still's energetic and resourceful leadership,"[28] asserts historian Benjamin Quarles. From his office and his private residence, Still coordinated escapes with Underground Railroad volunteers as far away as Virginia. He devoted most of the remainder of his waking hours to operating a sort of social services agency for newly arrived runaways in Philadelphia. By the mid-1850s, Still and his committee were assisting upward of sixty escaped slaves per month, providing them with anything from food and clothing to legal support, medical attention, and job counseling.

Over the years, Harriet Tubman would work closely with Still, whom she probably met through her Underground Railroad contacts soon after coming to Philadelphia in 1849. Still's assistance in locating safe houses, travel funds, and other types of aid was invaluable to Tubman in the planning and execution of her forays into the upper South. Once she had shepherded a new group of fugitives to Philadelphia, Tubman depended on Still and his committee to secure food, shelter, new clothing to replace their ragged slave garments, and, if they intended to remain in the city rather than push on to Canada, employment for her charges. In addition to being one of Tubman's key collaborators in the

William Still, Early Chronicler of the Underground Railroad

Almost without exception, William Still's office was the first place that the hundreds of fugitives who entered Philadelphia stopped each year during the decade before the Civil War. An historian at heart, Still maintained detailed records on every runaway who passed through his office from 1852 on. He carefully recorded information on their families, appearance, owners, escape routes, and the blacks and whites who helped them along their way north. By amazing coincidence, one of the more than six hundred fugitive slaves he interviewed turned out to be his older brother, Peter. He had been left behind in Maryland by the men's mother when she fled north to New Jersey a decade before William's birth in 1821.

Given the highly sensitive nature of his records, Still was careful to store them in a well-concealed spot, far from prying eyes. Shortly before the Civil War broke out, he transferred the documents from his office to the loft of a building in a Philadelphia cemetery. There they would remain until the Confederacy was defeated and slavery was finally outlawed throughout the

William Still recorded the histories of more than 600 fugitive slaves he helped on the Underground Railroad.

United States. In 1872, seven years after the end of the Civil War, Still published his records in an eight-hundred-page volume simply entitled *The Underground Railroad*. Still's book included personal narratives from hundreds of runaways as well as correspondence between Still and other Underground Railroad agents such as Thomas Garrett. It has proved invaluable to historians ever since and even today remains the most complete record of day-to-day Underground operations.

Underground Railroad, Still was also one of the indefatigable conductor's greatest admirers. "[A] woman of no pretensions, indeed, a more ordinary specimen of humanity could hardly be found among the most unfortunate farmhands of the South," Still wrote of his Underground colleague "Yet, in point of courage, shrewdness, and disinterested exertions to rescue her fellow-men, by making personal visits to Maryland among the slaves, she was without her equal."[29]

Aside from Still, the individual on whom Tubman relied most

Underground Railroad stationmaster Thomas Garrett frequently helped Tubman assist escaped slaves.

heavily in carrying out her missions of mercy was a white man—the legendary Underground stationmaster and abolitionist Thomas Garrett. A devout Quaker and prosperous merchant, Garrett first became involved in the antislavery movement about the time of Tubman's birth in the early 1820s. By the beginning of the Civil War, he had helped more than twenty-five hundred slaves from Delaware, Maryland, and Virginia attain their freedom, sheltering many of the fugitives in the back room of his store or in his three-story house in Wilmington, Delaware, a few miles from the Pennsylvania border. Tubman, who frequently stopped with her charges at Garrett's Shipley Street home, never hesitated to ask the stationmaster for the cash or other supplies that she needed to take her groups on to Philadelphia or all the way north to Ontario. Garrett, who admiringly referred to Tubman in his letters as "the colored heroine" and "that noble woman,"[30] was unfailingly generous with her. On one occasion, Garrett recalled, Tubman turned up at his door without warning and announced, "God has sent me to you for money." Garrett protested that he could not help her out this time because he had just given his last dollar to another group of fugitives. "You can give me what I need now, God never fools me,"[31] Harriet insisted. Suddenly, Garrett remembered the five pounds that a Scottish abolitionist group had recently sent him and promptly handed the donation to Tubman. Equal to about twenty-five dollars in American money, it was enough to fund a carriage trip to Philadelphia for Tubman and the pregnant fugitive in her care as well as another trip south to Maryland to rescue a young mother and her three children.

A Daring Christmas Mission

In December 1854, Tubman's devoted friends and benefactors in the Underground Railroad, Thomas Garrett and William Still, helped her achieve one of the most daring rescues of her Underground career. A few days before Christmas, Tubman set out from Philadelphia for Dr. Anthony C. Thompson's plantation near the Choptank River, the very place from which she had escaped five years earlier. Her mission was to spirit away her three brothers, Robert, Benjamin, and Henry, before their owner, Eliza Brodess, could put them on the auction block.

Ever since the death of Edward Brodess, Harriet's brothers, and particularly her younger siblings Benjamin and Henry, had feared that their debt-ridden mistress might sell them south at any moment. For whatever reason, however, Eliza Brodess kept putting off the brothers' sale. Finally in late 1854, she decided to auction off all three siblings right after Christmas, a popular time for masters in the upper South to rid themselves of their extra field hands. When Harriet got wind of Brodess's plans, she rushed south to lead Benjamin, Henry, and Robert Ross to freedom.

Before Tubman left Philadelphia, however, she asked an acquaintance to compose a letter for her to an Underground Railroad agent who lived in Tobacco Stick, not far from the plantation where her brothers were then working. Because the agent, a free black named Jacob Jackson, was already under suspicion for aiding

Living conditions for runaway slaves were difficult.

several runaways, Tubman had to be careful what she said in the letter. Encoded in the missive, which was signed with the name of Jackson's son, was an urgent message for Tubman's brothers: "Read my letter to the old folks, and give my love to them, and tell my brothers to be always *watching unto prayer*, and *when the good old ship Zion comes along, to be ready to step aboard.*"[32] Jackson, who had undoubtedly communicated with Tubman by this method before, understood that she was coming soon for her brothers and would meet them near the "old folks'" place—Ben and Rit Ross's cabin on Thompson's plantation. The timing of the escape was ideal because, as was customary in the antebellum South, Eliza Brodess allowed her slaves to spend Christmas Day with their relatives whenever possible, and the Ross brothers were already planning to travel to their parents' home for the holiday.

On Christmas Eve, Tubman, Henry, Benjamin, and four of the Ross brothers' friends met near Ben and Rit's cabin in an old corncrib, a building used to store corn for fodder. Robert, whose wife had just given birth to the couple's third child, did not show up until early Christmas morning. Leaving his family had been extremely difficult for Robert, but before he left, he promised his wife that Tubman or another Underground conductor would return soon for her and the children. After Robert's arrival, the eight fugitives decided to remain in the corncrib until nightfall, then start their long trek northward under the cover of darkness. Tubman had planned to conceal her bold rescue operation from her mother and father, knowing that her elderly parents were certain to be grilled later regarding their sons' disappearance. But hunger soon won out over caution, and one of the brothers' friends was sent to the Ross cabin to ask for food. Before entering the corncrib, Ben Ross tied a handkerchief over his eyes, so when he was interrogated later he could honestly declare that he had not seen any of his children that day.

When Tubman and her party reached Wilmington several days later, she immediately contacted Thomas Garrett. He presented the weary travelers with enough money to hire a carriage to Philadelphia and bought new shoes for Tubman and one of her passengers because they had completely worn out their old ones. Soon afterward, the fugitives arrived at William Still's office in Philadelphia, where they were given food, clothing, and money for train tickets. After changing trains in New York City, Albany, Rochester, and Buffalo with rests at various Underground stations along the way, Harriet Tubman and her flock finally arrived at Saint Catharines in early 1855. Although the Ross brothers would stay on in Canada, by the summer of 1855 Tubman had already made her way back to Philadelphia. Many of her loved ones still remained in bondage, and Tubman could not rest until she had shepherded them north, too, even though her defiant campaign of liberation meant jeopardizing her own freedom time and time again.

Chapter Four

"The Slaves Call Her Moses"

During the last half of the 1850s, Harriet Tubman slipped back into the South repeatedly to rescue dozens of her fellow African Americans from the chains of bondage. As Tubman's fame as an Underground Railroad conductor of remarkable daring and effectiveness grew, she faced increasing danger in her missions of mercy. Emboldened both by an unwavering confidence in God's protection and in the dedication of her Underground colleagues, during the five years leading up to the Civil War Tubman courageously journeyed to the slave states of Maryland, Virginia, and Delaware time and time again to lead family members, friends, and, in many instances, complete strangers to freedom.

A Steadfast Faith

The one thing about Harriet Tubman that seems to have most impressed her Underground Railroad colleagues was her apparent lack of concern for her own safety. "Great fears were entertained for her safety, but she seemed wholly devoid of personal fear," Thomas Garrett wrote of his secret collaborator. "The idea of being captured by slave-hunters or slave-holders seemed never to enter her mind."[33]

Tubman's remarkable courage in the face of danger was firmly rooted in her Christian faith. Convinced that God had ordained her rescue missions, she never doubted for a moment that he would safeguard her on her perilous forays into slave territory. Early in her career with the Underground Railroad, Tubman confided to a friend that God had appeared to her on three separate occasions to confirm her calling as a liberator of her fellow slaves:

Long ago when the Lord told me to go free my people, I said, "No, Lord! I can't go—don't ask me." But he came another time, I saw him just as plain. Then I said again, "Lord, go away—get some better educated person—get a person with more culture than I have; go away, Lord." But he came back the third time, and speaks to me just as he did to Moses, and he says, "Harriet, I want you." I knew then I must do what he bid me.[34]

Religious faith inspired and sustained many slaves and abolitionists, including Tubman. Here, blacks attend a prayer meeting.

God not only protected her but also guided her every step on her missions of liberation, Tubman believed. When many years later Sarah Bradford asked how it was possible that she had never lost a single passenger on her numerous journeys in and out of the slave South, Tubman replied: "Missus, it wasn't me, it was the Lord! I always told him, 'I trust to you. I don't know where to go or what to do, but I expect you to lead me,' and he always did."[35] According to another contemporary, during her long career with the Underground Railroad Tubman would often "talk about 'consulting with God,' . . . just as one would consult a friend upon matters of business."[36] On more than one occasion, fugitives traveling with Tubman reported that the conductor would suddenly stop as though listening to a voice only she could hear, then abruptly command her party to change direction. Later the run-

Harriet Tubman and the Daguerreotype

Harriet Tubman's career with the Underground Railroad during the 1850s coincided with the growing popularity in America of the daguerreotype, an early photographic print produced on a silver-coated copper plate. The increasingly widespread use of daguerreotypes in the United States during the decade before the Civil War was fortunate for Tubman because photography was to play a vital role in her secret operations. Since Tubman could not read, she was uncomfortable with presenting new Underground Railroad contacts with letters of introduction from mutual acquaintances. Yet, ever fearful of betrayal, Tubman was extremely wary of revealing her clandestine activities to anyone except another Underground operative. To protect against potentially dangerous mishaps, when she was on the road Tubman kept a collection of daguerreotypes of fellow agents and abolitionist friends with her at all times. If a hitherto unknown contact could identify the men and women in the photographs by name, Tubman felt confident that he or she was personally acquainted with her colleagues and could therefore be trusted.

aways would learn that they had just missed being ambushed by slave catchers.

Tubman's intense spirituality was hardly unusual. Christianity was a crucial source of strength and hope for hundreds of thousands of African Americans compelled to endure brutal punishments, grueling workloads, and all the other hardships and indignities of slave life. Slaveholders sought to use religion to control and intimidate their human property. Not surprisingly, one of their favorite biblical texts was the passage from Saint Paul's epistle to the Ephesians: "Servants, be obedient to them who are your masters according to the flesh, with fear and trembling, in singleness of your heart, as unto Christ" (Ephesians 6:5). African Americans remained unconvinced by their masters' efforts to make them feel inferior, however. All people—slave or free—were equal in the sight of the Lord, they insisted. Rejecting Southern white interpretations of the Bible, they fervently believed that God wanted all his children to be free. Just as God had delivered his chosen people, the Israelites, from enslavement by the Egyptians, African Americans looked forward to the day when they, too, would be delivered from the chains of bondage. "God's time is always near," Tubman once declared. "He set the North Star in the heavens; He gave me the strength in my limbs; He meant I should be *free*."[37]

A Meticulous Planner

If Tubman had faith that God would always shield her in her missions of deliverance, she still planned every detail of her operations with extreme care. In organizing and carrying out her perilous rescues, declared abolitionist Ednah Cheney, Tubman "has shown . . . all the characteristics of a great leader: courage, foresight, prudence, self-control, ingenuity, subtle perception, command over others' minds. Her nature is at once profoundly practical and highly imaginative."[38]

Like other successful Underground Railroad conductors, Harriet Tubman put a great deal of thought into the timing of her missions. She usually traveled south in the late fall or early winter when days were shorter and her parties could travel under the cover of darkness for more hours. Almost invariably, she started out with her flocks on a Saturday night. Sunday was the only day of the week when slaves were permitted to visit relatives on nearby plantations. Consequently, there was a good chance that any slave who sneaked off on a Saturday evening would not be missed until Monday morning, giving Tubman's party more than a twenty-four-hour head start on slave patrols and bounty hunters. And even if a slave's absence was noticed on Sunday, Tubman figured, because newspapers were never printed on the Sabbath, the owner could not take out an advertisement for his lost property until Monday at the earliest.

Perhaps keeping the old adage "God helps those who help themselves" in mind, Tubman took every possible precaution to avoid capture. According to her friend Ednah Cheney, when Tubman gathered her recruits for the hazardous journey north, she made a point of never being seen on any of the runaways' plantations herself, "but appointed a rendezvous for her company eight or ten miles [(13–16km)] distant, so that if they were discovered at the first start she was not compromised." Furthermore, noted Cheney, Tubman always tried to ensure that she "had confidential friends all along the road"[39]—typically Underground Railroad agents—who would help her obtain food, fresh water, or other necessities while her party stayed safely hidden in a nearby forest or swamp. If Underground volunteers were unavailable, Tubman would sometimes hire free blacks to assist her party. According to Cheney, it was not unusual for Tubman to pay a local freedman to shadow her charges' masters as they were posting reward notices and then tear the handbills down as soon as the owners had moved on.

Steely Nerves and a Gift for Theatrics

Carrying a loaded revolver was another important precaution that Tubman routinely took on her forays behind enemy lines. She brought along the pistol not only for protection against slave catchers but also to prevent any fainthearted followers from turning back. Convinced that the weakness of just one man or woman could jeopardize the entire party, Tubman preserved a strict military discipline among her charges. If she allowed a runaway to return home, Tubman worried, there was a good possibility that during the inevitable interrogation by authorities the slave would reveal critical secrets such as routes or the names of

Slaves were often transported in groups along the Underground Railroad.

Underground operatives. A dead fugitive could tell no tales, she reasoned. When Ednah Cheney heard about Harriet's harsh rule of "go on or die," she asked the conductor if she was actually capable of killing a nervous follower. Tubman replied coolly:

> Yes, if he was weak enough to give out, he'd be weak enough to betray us all, and all who had helped us; and do you think I would let so many die just for one coward man? . . . One time . . . a man gave out the second night; his feet were sore and swollen, he couldn't go any further; he'd rather go back and die, if he must. They tried all arguments in vain, bathed his feet, tried to strengthen him, but it was of no use, he would go back. . . . I told the boys to get their guns ready, and shoot him. They'd have done it in a minute; but when he heard that, he jumped right up and went on as well as anybody.[40]

Tubman's steely nerves were matched by her extraordinary inventiveness in overcoming a treacherous situation. A master of

Harriet Tubman and Her Musical Code

On her rescue missions, Harriet Tubman, who had a strong singing voice, often used familiar African American spirituals to communicate with her charges in a kind of secret code. She relied on the beloved songs to convey a host of hidden messages. For instance, according to Sarah Bradford, if after surveying the road ahead, Tubman determined that the coast was clear, she would signal to her passengers to come out of their hiding spots by singing:

> Hail, oh hail ye happy spirits,
> Death no more shall make you fear,
> No grief nor sorrow, pain nor anguish
> Shall no more distress you there.

If Tubman spotted potential danger ahead, however, she would warn her flock to remain concealed by singing the old spiritual:

> Go down, Moses,
> Way down into Egypt land.
> Tell old Pharaoh
> Let my people go.

Far from being unique to Harriet Tubman, the use of coded spirituals to transmit messages was a long-standing practice among slaves in the antebellum South. One traditional spiritual, "Follow the Drinking Gourd," served as a sort of simple map for runaways headed north, with its allusions to the Big Dipper constellation and the North Star. Another hymn, "Steal Away," became particularly popular as a coded encouragement to other slaves to flee, or steal away, to the North and freedom:

> Steal away, steal away
> Steal away to Jesus,
> Steal away, steal away
> I ain't got long to stay here.

Quoted in Sarah Bradford, *Harriet Tubman: The Moses of Her People*, 1886. Reprint, New York: Carol, 1994, pp. 36–38.

disguise, Tubman also possessed a natural gift for theatrics. "She seems to have command over her face, and can banish all expression from her features, and look so stupid that nobody would suspect her of knowing enough to be dangerous,"[41] observed one admiring contemporary.

During her career with the Underground Railroad, Tubman's acting skills helped her emerge unscathed from more than one tight spot. When on one of her operations she boldly decided to visit a market near a former master's farm to purchase food for her party, she found herself virtually face-to-face with the farmer himself. Without missing a beat, she pulled her sunbonnet low over her face and adopted the slow, stooped gait of an elderly person. Then Tubman stealthily pinched the legs of the two live chickens she was carrying. Immediately, the birds began to flutter about wildly. As the farmer passed just inches away from his onetime slave, all he noticed was a flustered old woman trying to keep her family's dinner from getting away. On another occasion when she visited her old home, Tubman spied a former employer sitting near her on a train. Tubman quickly grabbed a newspaper and pretended to be absorbed in it. Her master was bound to remember that like the vast majority of slaves, she was illiterate, and would never suspect the true identity of the woman behind the newspaper, Tubman figured. Her ruse worked, and she made it to her destination without incident.

Tubman Rescues Her Parents

In June 1857, Tubman embarked on what may have been her riskiest operation ever: retrieving her elderly parents from the Eastern Shore. By this time, Tubman and her exploits were well-known to Eastern Shore slaveholders and authorities, and her friends in the Underground Railroad worried that another visit to her old neighborhood would be pushing her luck. Indeed, Maryland slave owners were so eager to put a stop to Tubman's rescue operations that they had recently raised the price on her head to twelve thousand dollars—well over one hundred thousand dollars in today's money.

Tubman did not set off on her hazardous mission to the Eastern Shore in the summer of 1857 to liberate her parents from slavery; by the mid-1850s, both Ben and Rit Ross were legally free. Manumitted over a decade earlier by the will of his master, Anthony Thompson, Ben finally managed to scrape together enough money in 1855 to buy Rit's freedom from Eliza Brodess. Despite her parents' free status, however, Tubman was extremely anxious to get them out of Maryland. She had heard through the Underground grapevine that Ben was in imminent danger of being arrested because he was suspected of aiding several runaways. In fact, that March Ben had briefly hidden a group of eight fugitives in his house.

Tubman realized that the long trip north was bound to be grueling for her parents and that escaping Maryland by foot was almost certainly beyond their physical capabilities. "She also knew that the short nights of summer presented danger. But she ignored her worries as she prepared for a June expedition—the only rescue operation of hers known to have taken place in summer,"[42] notes historian Catherine Clinton.

Resolved to make the journey north as easy as possible on her aging mother and father, upon arriving in the Eastern Shore Tubman purchased a horse and two old carriage wheels on an axle. She then fashioned a primitive buggy by laying a board across the axle for a seat and hitching the horse to the contraption with a rope and a straw collar. Traveling only at night, Tubman managed to get her parents as far as northern Delaware in the makeshift rig. When she reached Wilmington, Tubman promptly contacted Thomas Garrett. As usual, the famous stationmaster came through for his Underground colleague, providing Harriet and her parents with enough money to purchase train tickets all the way through to Saint Catharines, where most of Tubman's siblings now resided.

"The Greatest Heroine of the Age"

Although Ben and Rit were happy to be reunited with their sons and other relatives in Saint Catharines, they suffered greatly during the frigid Canadian winters. For the sake of her parents' health, Harriet Tubman decided that she must find a home for them further south. In 1859, Senator William H. Seward, an ardent supporter of the antislavery movement, heard about Tubman's dilemma and generously offered to sell her a house and seven acres of land in his central New York hometown of Auburn

Senator William H. Seward sold Tubman a house in Auburn, New York, for her parents. An abolitionist, he charged her far less than market value for the property.

for just over one thousand dollars. Since Auburn had a large abolitionist community, Tubman felt confident that her parents would be as safe there as anywhere in the United States.

Seward's asking price for his house and land was well below market value, yet Tubman struggled to meet the payments on her mortgage debt. In order to fulfill her financial commitments to the senator, support her aging parents, and raise funds for future rescue missions, Tubman concluded that she had no choice but to take some time off from her Underground Railroad work for fund-raising. Spurred on by her many friends and admirers within the abolitionist movement, she decided to join the popular antislavery lecture circuit in the Northeast.

William Wells Brown:
Underground Railroad Conductor Novelist

◼

During the late 1850s, when she was a speaker on the Northeastern anti-slavery lecture circuit, Harriet Tubman had the opportunity to meet and often share the stage with other leading African American abolitionists. One of the most famous of these black antislavery activists was William Wells Brown.

Brown, a mulatto, was born about 1814 on a plantation in Kentucky. His mother was a slave, and his father was a relative of his owner. When Brown was a child, his master relocated to Saint Louis, Missouri. In January 1834, Brown escaped from his owner and made his way north. He worked as a boatman on Lake Erie, and smuggled runaway slaves to Canada by hiding them on his steamboat. Charismatic and well-spoken, Brown was hired by the Western New York Anti-Slavery Society as a lecturer during the early 1840s. By 1847, he was lecturing for the Massachusetts Anti-Slavery Society and had published a best-selling autobiography, *Narrative of William Wells Brown, a Fugitive Slave, Written By Himself.* Brown's book became the most popular slave narrative in the United States and England after Frederick Douglass's celebrated autobiography. In 1853, the self-taught Brown became the first African American to publish a novel when his *Clotel; or the President's Daughter*, whose central character was a runaway slave, first appeared in print in England.

William Wells Brown, the first African American to publish a novel, was an Underground Railroad conductor.

Tubman was an instant sensation on the abolitionist lecture circuit. Audiences were enthralled by the stories of her Underground exploits and responded generously to the request for donations that inevitably followed each of her talks. After hearing Tubman speak in Massachusetts in June 1859, antislavery activist Thomas Wentworth Higginson wrote enthusiastically to his mother:

We have had the greatest heroine of the age here, Harriet Tubman, a black woman, and a fugitive slave. . . . Her tales of adventure are beyond anything in fiction and her ingenuity and generalship are extraordinary. . . . [T]he slaves call her Moses. She has had a reward of twelve thousand dollars offered for her in Maryland and will probably be burned alive whenever she is caught, which she probably will be, first or last, as she is going again.[43]

A Successful Rescue Mission and a Failed One

In the spring of 1860 what Thomas Wentworth Higginson had lauded as Harriet Tubman's "extraordinary" ingenuity and generalship were clear evidence when she carried out her first-ever public rescue. On April 27, 1860, Tubman was passing through Troy, New York, when she heard that a fugitive slave by the name of Charles Nalle was being held in the federal commissioner's office in the heart of town. Determined to help Nalle, Tubman hurried to the commissioner's office, where she discovered that a large crowd of protesters had already gathered. Wrapping her shawl around her head and adopting the stooped posture of an elderly woman, she managed to slip into the building and make her way into the very room where Nalle's case was being heard. When she learned that the sheriff was about to escort Nalle to a nearby judge's office, she ran to the window and alerted the crowd below that the prisoner was on his way out.

What happened next clearly demonstrated that if Tubman had been able to participate in abolitionist John Brown's paramilitary operation the previous October, she would have proven herself a fearless and skilled warrior at Harpers Ferry. As Nalle was being led out of the building, Tubman suddenly grabbed the fugitive by the wrists, holding on doggedly while the sheriff and his deputies punched her and hit her with their billy clubs. Bruised and bloody, her clothing in shreds, Tubman finally managed to pry the prisoner loose from his captors. She then turned Nalle over to the crowd, who rushed him down to the docks to be rowed across the Hudson River to West Troy. But Nalle's—and Tubman's—ordeal was not over yet; after Nalle was recaptured by lawmen in West Troy, Tubman had to come to his rescue once again. Dodging bullets, she bravely led a band of mostly black

Even after escaping to freedom, African Americans faced lives of poverty and discrimination.

townspeople in an all-out assault on the building where Nalle was being detained. After a vicious fight, Tubman and her followers finally managed to get Nalle away in a wagon that they had commandeered.

A little more than six months after her rescue of Charles Nalle, Harriet Tubman embarked on what was to be her final mission for the Underground Railroad. For years she had been trying to get her sister Rachel and Rachel's two children out of the Eastern Shore. Complicating her efforts was the fact that Rachel's son and daughter lived more than 10 miles (16km) away from their mother, and Rachel adamantly refused to leave Maryland without them. In December 1860, at great risk to herself, Tubman returned to Dorchester County one more time to retrieve her sibling and her family. Tragically, soon after arriving in Maryland, Tubman discovered that Rachel had died. Her grief at the loss of her sister was compounded when she failed to rendezvous with her niece and nephew in a forest near their plantation.

Determined that her trip behind enemy lines should not be wasted, Tubman brought seven other slaves north that December, including an infant who had to be drugged with opium to keep it from crying and revealing the fugitives' hiding places. Unexpectedly cold, wet weather made the journey particularly arduous for everyone involved. Tubman, who had never fully recovered from the head wound she suffered as a teenager, returned to Auburn in fragile health. The last ten years had taken an enormous toll on her, and, with most of her family now settled in the North, she decided the time had finally come to end her career as an Underground Railroad conductor. Harriet Tubman's devotion to abolishing the cruel institution of slavery in her homeland, however, remained as powerful as ever.

Chapter Five

"To Take Care of My People"

By the end of 1860, when Tubman made her final trip south on the Underground Railroad, the United States was heading rapidly toward civil war. In November the election of Abraham Lincoln as president had ignited a full-blown secession crisis. Fearful that the election of a Northerner opposed to the expansion of slavery into the territories would lead to the outlawing of slavery throughout the nation, by Lincoln's inauguration on March 4, 1861, seven Southern states had seceded (withdrawn) from the Union and formed the Confederate States of America. Barely a month later, the Civil War erupted after Confederate forces fired on the federal garrison at Fort Sumter in Charleston, South Carolina, and four more Southern states abandoned the Union.

In common with other Underground Railroad and abolitionist leaders, Harriet Tubman welcomed the war, convinced that it would finally bring about the downfall of American slavery. At great risk to herself, she journeyed south once again to aid the federal forces in their long and bloody struggle against the Confederacy. Yet even after the Union victory in April 1865 and the abolition of slavery throughout the United States, Tubman's commitment to the advancement of her fellow African Americans would remain steadfast. When God first commanded her "to go free my people" following her own escape from bondage, he had not meant her to do his bidding for just a day or a week. Tubman told an interviewer more than two decades after the war's end: "No! The Lord who told me to take care of my people meant me to do it just so long as I live, and so I do what he told me to."[44]

Port Royal

Historians can only speculate regarding Tubman's whereabouts during the first months of the Civil War, but by late 1861 she was definitely in Boston, where she met with the abolitionist governor of Massachusetts, John Andrew. A great admirer of Tubman's work with the Underground Railroad, Andrew was convinced that her experience with undercover missions would be of tremendous value to the Union war effort. In the spring of 1862, Andrew arranged for Tubman to travel to the Union-occupied Sea Islands off coastal South Carolina to assist newly freed slaves and to "operate within the enemy's lines in procuring information and scouts."[45] The headquarters for her covert operations was to be the town of Beaufort on Port Royal Island, just south of Charleston Harbor.

When Tubman first arrived at Beaufort, however, her focus was not on scouting or spying behind enemy lines. Instead, she devoted most of her time to ministering to the hundreds of freed slaves who had once toiled on Port Royal's vast cotton plantations and the steady stream of runaways who found their

Massachusetts governor John Andrew helped Tubman travel to the Sea Islands off the South Carolina coast, where she aided escaped slaves and spied for the North.

way to the island from the Confederate-controlled mainland. Lacking employment, land, houses, or schools of their own, the former slaves lived in desperate poverty. Tubman's humanitarian efforts on Port Royal included distributing clothing and supplies from Northern charitable organizations to ex-slaves and tending to the sick and injured at the refugee hospital. She also took it upon herself to assist recently freed bondwomen in making the transition from forced labor to wage labor. Using two hundred dollars of her own money, Tubman arranged for a large wash-

In this 1862 photo, freed slaves gather on a Union-occupied plantation in South Carolina. Tubman helped many slaves make the transition to freedom while in South Carolina.

house to be built where she could train former field hands to be laundresses. Her purpose in this undertaking, she later explained, was to encourage the women to help support themselves by taking in washing and mending for the troops "instead of depending wholly on Government aid"[46] to survive.

Recruitment of Black Soldiers

Shortly after Tubman settled in Port Royal, two events occurred in the nation's capital that heartened her enormously. The first took place late in the summer of 1862, when Congress finally approved the recruitment of black soldiers. Despite strong abolitionist support for using black manpower in the war effort, the Lincoln administration had stubbornly refused to allow African Americans in the military. He did so largely to placate loyal slave-holding states like Kentucky and Missouri. After a series of Union defeats in 1861 and 1862, the federal government realized that the war was not going to be as easily or as quickly won as they had originally hoped and that they needed all the extra manpower they could get. Consequently, they began to view black military service in a more favorable light. In August 1862, Tubman and other antislavery activists were elated when the military governor of the Department of the South (as the Union-held areas in South Carolina, Georgia, and Florida were called) was officially authorized to raise five regiments of African American troops on the Sea Islands. The regiments' chief assignment was to help break the back of the Confederacy by carrying out raiding missions into nearby rebel territory and bringing away valuable enemy property, particularly slaves.

About four months after the federal government empowered the Department of the South to recruit black soldiers on the Sea Islands, a second event occurred in Washington that Tubman found deeply gratifying: President Lincoln issued his Emancipation Proclamation. The scope of the proclamation fell far short of the expectations of Tubman and other abolitionist leaders. For example, although the edict declared all slaves within the Confederacy free, it did not emancipate any slaves in the loyal border states of Maryland, Kentucky, or Missouri. Because the proclamation officially made the war a contest for freedom as well as to save the Union, however, when Lincoln's decree became law on

January 1, 1863, antislavery activists and former slaves through-out the United States rejoiced, including on Port Royal. Tubman almost certainly attended the island's huge Emancipation Day celebration. There, a former Port Royal planter who had manu-mitted his slaves twenty-five years earlier read the proclamation aloud to a crowd of some four thousand, mostly African Ameri-can listeners.

The Combahee River Raid

By the time that the Emancipation Proclamation became law, Tubman was anxious to participate more directly in the Northern military effort. After all, she had come to Port Royal not only to assist newly liberated slaves but also to act as a spy and scout behind Confederate lines. The former Underground Railroad conductor could not help but feel that her talents and experience were being underutilized. Fortunately for Tubman and the Union war effort, several military officials in the Department of the South shared her concerns, and during the winter of 1863 she was finally authorized to form her own intelligence service to assist her in infiltrating and mapping out the South Carolinian interior.

By the spring of 1863, Tubman had assembled a small but highly effective spy ring of seven local men, all of them ex-slaves. Two were former boatmen who were intimately familiar with the waterways that Union raiders from the Sea Islands used to reach the Confederate-held interior from the coast. The most famous and significant operation that Tubman and her men helped to plan—the Combahee River raid—took place on one of those waterways just south of Charleston on the night of June 2, 1863.

Shortly before midnight on June 2, three federal gunboats qui-etly departed Port Royal for the mouth of the nearby Combahee River and rebel territory. On board were 150 troops from the all-black Second South Carolina Volunteers, their white commanding officer, Colonel James Montgomery, and stationed in the lookout of the lead ship, Harriet Tubman herself. Using the intelligence that she and her scouts had gathered from local blacks during the days and weeks leading up to the raid, Tubman was able to guide the gunboats safely around the Confederate mines that lurked below the river's surface. She was also able to show the pilots

2nd South Carolina Volunteer Infantry (colored) take the oath of allegiance. They participated in the Combahee River Raid.

exactly where to stop to pick up the hundreds of fugitive slaves hidden along the shoreline that night and to drop off the landing parties assigned to torch and plunder rebel stockpiles and warehouses. Under Tubman's skillful leadership, by dawn the Union raiders had spirited away almost eight hundred irreplaceable field workers and ravaged the area's largest plantations, all without losing a single soldier. The official Confederate account of the raid highlighted the critical role of Tubman and her spies in planning and executing the operation: "The enemy seems to have been well posted as to the character and capacity of [Confederate] troops and their small chance of encountering opposition, and to have been well guided by persons thoroughly acquainted with the river and country,"[47] the report's author observed.

News of the Combahee River raid sped through the Union grapevine, and the War Department exalted over the daring operation's

In this illustration, members of the all-black 54th Regiment attack Fort Wagner in South Carolina. Tubman nursed many soldiers who were wounded in the battle.

success. Soon Northern newspapers had picked up on the story. Journalists were intrigued by the novel idea of a woman—and a black woman at that—leading a major military raid deep into enemy territory. In late June, a newspaper article by a Northern reporter who had witnessed the raiders' victorious return to Port Royal alluded to Tubman's key role in the expedition while preserving her anonymity: "Col. Montgomery and his gallant band of . . . black soldiers, *under the guidance of a black woman,* dashed into the enemy's country, struck a bold and effective blow, destroying millions of dollars worth of commissary store, cotton, and lordly dwellings, and striking terror into the heart of rebeldom brought off near 800 slaves and thousands of dollars worth of property, without losing a man or receiving a scratch."[48] The following month, Franklin Sanborn referred to Tubman by name in an article for the antislavery periodical the *Boston Commonwealth*, which not only lauded her leadership in the Combahee raid but also her many contributions to the Underground Railroad before the war.

"It Was the Dead That We Reaped"

Just weeks after the Combahee River raid, Tubman found herself aiding the Union cause in the less glorious but crucial role of army nurse in what was to become one of the war's best-known battles: the assault on Fort Wagner by the all-black Massachusetts Fifty-fourth Infantry Regiment. Shortly after issuing the Emancipation Proclamation in January 1863, Lincoln had given Governor John Andrew permission to form the Massachusetts Fifty-fourth, the very first Union regiment to be comprised of free blacks from the Northern states. Although abolitionists of both races enthusiastically welcomed the regiment's creation, many Northern whites had grave doubts regarding the ability of black troops to hold up in combat. In mid-July, the men of the Fifty-fourth would more than prove their mettle when they led the charge against the heavily defended Confederate stronghold of Fort Wagner at the mouth of Charleston Harbor.

On July 18, as Tubman watched from nearby Beaufort, the Fifty-fourth Regiment valiantly scaled Fort Wagner's parapets under a withering barrage of enemy rifle and cannon fire. Although the regiment was ultimately forced to retreat, the men's exceptional sacrifice and bravery that day in Charleston Harbor was indisputable: Almost half of the Fifty-fourth's 650 members were killed or wounded in the assault. Tubman, who assisted in the grim task of retrieving the dead for burial as well as nursing the injured, eloquently described the battle and its horrific aftermath many years later: "And then we saw the lightning, and that was the guns; and then we heard the thunder, and that was the big guns; and then we heard the rain falling, and that was the drops of blood falling; and when we came to get in the crops, it was the dead that we reaped."[49]

For nearly a year after the bloody assault on Fort Wagner, Tubman remained on the Sea Islands, acting as a nurse and cook to the Union troops stationed there while also continuing her covert activities as a scout and spy in the Southern interior. After having been away from home for nearly three years, during the summer of 1864 Tubman finally requested a leave of absence from her duties in South Carolina to visit her elderly parents in New York. As it turned out, she would not return south until the Civil War was nearly over.

The End of the War

Back in Auburn, the exhausting pace she had maintained at Port Royal finally caught up with Tubman. The periodic drowsy spells that had plagued her ever since her head injury nearly three decades earlier grew more frequent and intense, and for months Harriet was virtually confined to her bed. Not until March of 1865 did she feel well enough to resume her work for the Union war effort. Rather than return to the Sea Islands, however, Tubman decided to serve as a nurse at Fort Monroe, Virginia, where she had heard that the military hospitals were severely understaffed.

On April 9, 1865, the Confederate army under General Robert E. Lee surrendered at Appomattox Court House following four devastating years of war. Tubman stayed on in Fort Monroe for several more months to care for the long struggle's last casualties. In July she traveled to Washington, D.C., to report on the deplorable conditions in Virginia's understaffed and inadequately supplied veteran's hospitals and to secure back pay for her wartime services as a nurse, cook, spy, and scout, work for which she had received only two hundred dollars in compensation from the army. Although several high-ranking civilian and military officials wrote letters attesting to her valuable contributions to the Union effort, over the years Congress repeatedly denied Tubman's requests for her lost wages or for a veteran's pension. Some of Tubman's friends in Auburn blamed the federal government's failure to compensate her for her wartime service on the fact that she had never held an official commission from the army. As far as Tubman was concerned, however, Washington had no excuse for what she considered its shoddy treatment of her: "You wouldn't think that after I served the flag so faithfully I should come to want under its folds,"[50] she observed bitterly to an acquaintance.

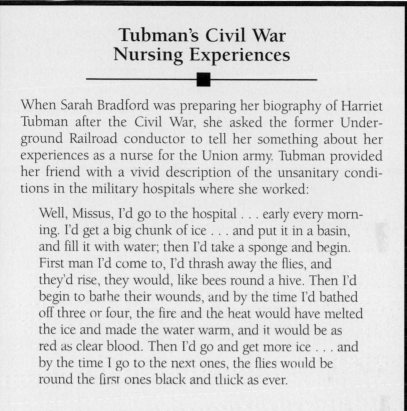

Tubman's Civil War Nursing Experiences

When Sarah Bradford was preparing her biography of Harriet Tubman after the Civil War, she asked the former Underground Railroad conductor to tell her something about her experiences as a nurse for the Union army. Tubman provided her friend with a vivid description of the unsanitary conditions in the military hospitals where she worked:

> Well, Missus, I'd go to the hospital . . . early every morning. I'd get a big chunk of ice . . . and put it in a basin, and fill it with water; then I'd take a sponge and begin. First man I'd come to, I'd thrash away the flies, and they'd rise, they would, like bees round a hive. Then I'd begin to bathe their wounds, and by the time I'd bathed off three or four, the fire and the heat would have melted the ice and made the water warm, and it would be as red as clear blood. Then I'd go and get more ice . . . and by the time I go to the next ones, the flies would be round the first ones black and thick as ever.

Quoted in Sarah Bradford, *Harriet Tubman: The Moses of Her People.* 1886. Reprint, New York: Carol, 1994, pp. 97.

Deeply discouraged and all but penniless, Tubman headed back home to Auburn in the fall of 1865. As she soon discovered, in the postwar North as in the South, discrimination against African Americans lingered on. While Tubman was traveling from Philadelphia to New York, a racist train conductor ordered her to give up her seat in the passenger car. When she stubbornly refused to budge, the conductor called on three other men to assist him in forcibly removing her. Together, they dragged Tubman out of her seat and hurled her into the baggage car, badly wrenching her arm and shoulder in the process.

Money Worries

Tubman's sprained arm and shoulder troubled her for many months after she arrived home in Auburn. But she had little time to convalesce from her injuries. In order to support herself and her elderly parents, she was soon putting in long workdays. When she was not cooking, cleaning, or babysitting for her neighbors, Tubman was growing vegetables to sell door-to-door. Although she earned barely enough to feed and clothe herself and her parents from these endeavors, Tubman's door was always open to anyone in need, and her house soon became a sort of informal shelter for the neediest members of

Sojourner Truth: Abolitionist, Feminist, and Preacher

During the summer of 1864, less than a year before the end of the Civil War, Harriet Tubman finally crossed paths with the other most famous African American woman of her era, Sojourner Truth. The two antislavery activists

Like Tubman, abolitionist Sojourner Truth was a powerful speaker. The two met in 1864.

met at the train station in Boston. Like Tubman, Truth was the child of enslaved parents. Originally named Isabella Baumfree, she was born in rural New York about 1797, when slavery was still legal in the state. Carrying her infant daughter with her, in 1826 Baumfree fled from her abusive master, just months before slavery was outlawed in New York. By 1830, she had settled in New York City, where she soon became a popular preacher. In 1843, Baumfree changed her name to Sojourner Truth because, she later explained, God had called her to travel through the country to preach his truth. Like Tubman, Truth was an orator of tremendous skill and power even though she was illiterate. During the two decades leading up to the Civil War, Truth lectured all over the North on her three favorite subjects: Christianity, abolitionism, and women's rights.

her race, including disabled Civil War veterans, orphans, and the elderly.

Generous to a fault, Tubman was chronically short on funds. Her method of managing her finances was "to give away all the money she had on her at the moment and trust to the Lord to fill the void,"[51] noted one admiring yet obviously exasperated acquaintance. Determined to find a way to help her, in 1868 Tubman's old Underground Railroad and abolitionist friends decided to have a book published about the celebrated conductor, with all the profits from the sale of the volume to be donated to Tubman herself. Sarah Bradford, a local author and friend of Tubman's, volunteered to write the biography, and several wealthy donors covered the printing costs.

Although Bradford spent many hours interviewing Tubman for her biography, modern scholars have questioned the book's accuracy on a number of points. For example, most of Tubman's recent biographers believe that Bradford exaggerated the number of slaves that Harriet brought north between 1850 and 1860. Perhaps for dramatic effect, Bradford claimed that Tubman took nineteen separate trips south during the 1850s and personally rescued more than three hundred people from bondage. Today, most historians agree that Tubman made thirteen or fourteen trips into slave territory before the Civil War and personally escorted between one hundred and two hundred blacks north. Tubman, who remained illiterate all her life, never maintained a written record of her expeditions for the Underground Railroad, and in later interviews with reporters or biographers, she appeared to have no clear recollection of her various missions' dates or sequence.

Remarriage, Widowhood, and the Women's Rights Movement

In March 1869, the same year Bradford's biography, *Scenes in the Life of Harriet Tubman*, appeared in print, Harriet Tubman married for the second time. Not quite two years earlier, her unfaithful first husband, John Tubman, had been shot to death by a white neighbor in Maryland following an argument. Nelson Davis, Harriet Tubman's new spouse, was a Civil War veteran and former slave who had fled North Carolina for New York during

In this photo, Tubman (far left) and her second husband, Nelson Davis (third from left) pose with a group of slaves that she helped escape.

the late 1850s. Although he was at least two decades younger than Harriet Tubman, Davis suffered from tuberculosis, a serious lung disease, and his health remained fragile throughout most of their nineteen-year-long marriage.

Davis finally succumbed to his long illness in 1888. Two years later, Congress passed a law giving a small monthly pension to widows of Civil War veterans. Tubman was granted eight dollars a month for life, a sum that was eventually raised to twenty dollars a month. Tubman, who was now in her seventies, could have settled back and lived comfortably off her widow's pension and the proceeds from the sale of a revised edition of Bradford's biography that came out in 1886 under the title *Harriet Tubman: The Moses of Her People*. But that would not have been her way.

After her husband's death, Tubman took an increasingly active role in the women's rights movement, lecturing frequently at suffragist gatherings throughout New York and New England during

A Reporter's Impressions of Harriet Tubman in 1896

◼

When Harriet Tubman, who would have been in her seventies at the time, spoke before a women's suffrage convention in Upstate New York in 1896, a journalist from the newspaper the *Rochester Democrat* was in the audience. From his article, it is evident that the reporter was clearly impressed by Tubman. If Tubman made any specific reference to women's rights in her speech that day, however, he neglected to mention it in his piece.

> The old woman was once a slave, and as she stood before the assemblage in her cheap black gown and coat and big black straw bonnet without adornment, . . . she impressed one with the venerable dignity of her appearance. . . .
>
> She told of her escape from slavery in the south, choosing the doubtful experiment of liberty rather than submit to being sold to a new master. A big price was put on her head, and she came North, where she became one of the strongest workers for the underground railroad. . . .
>
> She told touchingly of the soldiers of the war and how she ministered to their mangled bodies. In her humility she considered it a great favor that these men should long for her to speak to them a kindly word, or offer them a drink, or wash and dress their wounds. . . .
>
> This old woman who can neither read nor write, has still a mission, which is the moral advancement of her race.

Harriet Tubman continued public speaking well into her 70s. This photo was taken around 1890.

Quoted in Jean M. Humez, *Harriet Tubman: The Life and the Life Stories*. Madison: University of Wisconsin Press, 2003, pp. 319–20.

the 1890s. She had known Susan B. Anthony and many of the suffragist movement's other leaders, most of whom had been fervent abolitionists, since her Underground Railroad days. Like Anthony, Tubman was dismayed by the fact that the Fifteenth Amendment to the Constitution, which was ratified in 1870, only granted African American men the right to vote while completely ignoring the voting rights of women, black or white.

Tubman was widely admired by her fellow suffragists, who viewed her as nothing less than "a living embodiment of female ability and equal achievement,"[52] contends historian Jean Humez. In 1896, Tubman was a featured speaker at the first annual convention of the National Association of Colored Women, which was dedicated not only to gaining the vote but also to addressing the tremendous challenges faced by the nation's many impoverished black women, especially working mothers. Over the course of the next two years, Tubman was also formally honored by two predominantly white women's rights organizations, the New England Woman Suffrage Association and the Woman's State Association of New York.

The Harriet Tubman Home

Although Tubman remained deeply committed to the national women's rights crusade, during the final years of her life the cause that was closest to her heart was centered in her own central New York community. Since the end of the Civil War, Tubman's modest house in Auburn had served as an informal asylum for aged, sick, and disabled African Americans of both sexes. Before she died, Tubman was determined to found a charitable institution in Auburn to carry on her efforts on behalf of the elderly and infirm of her race. The need for such an establishment was urgent, she believed, because few charitable institutions in New York—or anywhere in the United States for that matter—were willing to admit blacks during the late nineteenth century.

In 1896, Tubman obtained a mortgage loan from a local bank and purchased a parcel of property next to her house for $1,450 that included a ten-room brick building and 25 acres (10ha.) of land. Tubman was convinced she had found the perfect location for her new charitable institution. Over the next several years, she struggled to scrape together enough money to staff and equip her pet project.

By 1903, Tubman had concluded that she would never be able to raise the money required to turn her dream into reality. That year she decided to donate the property she had purchased seven years earlier to Auburn's African Methodist Episcopal Zion Church, with the stipulation that it be converted as soon as possible into a facility "for aged and indigent colored people."[53] Five years later, the church had finally raised sufficient funds to get the institution up and running, and on June 23, 1908, the Harriet Tubman Home officially opened its doors.

The Harriet Tubman Home in Auburn, New York, was originally dedicated as a home for aged and infirm blacks. Today it is a memorial to Tubman's life and work.

When she was about 90 years old, Tubman moved into the home that bore her name.

Devotion to Duty

In May 1911, Harriet Tubman, now somewhere in the vicinity of ninety years old, moved into the caregiving facility that bore her name. A little less than two years later, on March 10, 1913, Harriet died of pneumonia. Shortly before breathing her last breath, Tubman sought to comfort the grieving family members and friends who had gathered around her by reciting a passage from the New Testament: "I go away to prepare a place for you, and where I am you may be also."[54]

On March 13, most of the town of Auburn—black and white—attended funeral services for Tubman at the African Methodist Episcopal Zion Church. A year later, Auburn's citizens turned out en masse again to pay homage to Harriet Tubman when a large bronze plaque honoring her memory was placed on the county courthouse. At the memorial ceremony, the celebrated black educator Booker T. Washington delivered the keynote address, praising Tubman for her lifelong "devotion to duty."[55]

Harriet Tubman's unyielding "devotion to duty" was indeed remarkable. With little thought for her own safety or comfort, Tubman dedicated herself to defeating the Confederacy and bringing about the demise of slavery throughout the United

States as a Civil War spy, scout, and nurse. Continuing her self-less campaign for the social, economic, and political advancement of her fellow African Americans after the war, she labored tirelessly for the poor, old, and forgotten of her race.

Yet Tubman's extraordinary spirit of self-sacrifice and commitment to racial justice were nowhere more evident than in her long and celebrated career with the Underground Railroad. As an Underground conductor of monumental daring and perseverance, Tubman jeopardized her own hard-won freedom time and time again to deliver relatives, friends, and total strangers from bondage. Unquestionably the Underground Railroad's most famous volunteer, Tubman may also have been its single most effective agent, courageously shepherding at least one hundred slaves to liberty during the decade leading up to the Civil War. With the exception of the radical abolitionist and freedom fighter John Brown, wrote Frederick Douglass to his friend and former Underground colleague, Harriet Tubman, in 1868, "I know of no one who has willingly encountered more perils and hardships to serve our enslaved people than you have."[56] Through her unwavering devotion to guiding others to liberty along the Underground Railroad, Harriet Tubman became one of black freedom's greatest champions and probably accomplished as much as any other individual in the history of the United States to undermine the brutal institution of slavery.

Notes

Chapter One: Born into Slavery

1. Catherine Clinton, *Harriet Tubman: The Road to Freedom.* New York: Little, Brown, 2004, p. 16.
2. Quoted in Kate Clifford Larson, *Bound for the Promised Land: Harriet Tubman, Portrait of an American Hero.* New York: Ballantine, 2004, p. 20.
3. Larson, *Bound for the Promised Land*, pp. 36–37.
4. Quoted in Larson, *Bound for the Promised Land*, p. 38.
5. Quoted in Fergus M. Bordewich, *Bound for Canaan: The Underground Railroad and the War for the Soul of America.* New York: HarperCollins, 2005, p. 347.
6. Sarah Bradford, *Harriet Tubman: The Moses of Her People.* 1886. Reprint, New York: Carol, 1994, p. 19.
7. Bradford, *Harriet Tubman*, pp. 20–21.
8. Quoted in Jean M. Humez, *Harriet Tubman: The Life and the Life Stories.* Madison: University of Wisconsin Press, 2003, p. 208.
9. Quoted in Larson, *Bound for the Promised Land*, p. 40.
10. Quoted in Bradford, *Harriet Tubman*, p. 21.
11. Quoted in Bradford, *Harriet Tubman*, p. 15.
12. Quoted in Larson, *Bound for the Promised Land*, p. 29.
13. Quoted in Bordewich, *Bound for Canaan*, p. 347.
14. Quoted in Humez, *Harriet Tubman*, pp. 13–14.

Chapter Two: "Liberty, or Death"

15. Quoted in Humez, *Harriet Tubman*, p. 25.
16. Quoted in Clinton, *Harriet Tubman*, p. 22.
17. Quoted in Humez, *Harriet Tubman*, p. 177.
18. Quoted in Humez, *Harriet Tubman*, p. 176.
19. Quoted in Charles L. Blockson, *The Underground Railroad: First-Person Narratives of Escapes to Freedom in the North.* Upper Saddle River, NJ: Prentice Hall, 1987, p. 118.
20. Quoted in Larson, *Bound for the Promised Land*, p. 78.
21. Quoted in Bradford, *Harriet Tubman*, p. 29.
22. Bordewich, *Bound for Canaan*, p. 349.

Chapter Three: Conductor on the Underground Railroad

23. Quoted in Bradford, *Harriet Tubman*, p. 30.
24. Quoted in Bradford, *Harriet Tubman*, pp. 31–32.
25. Quoted in Blockson, *The Under-*

ground Railroad, p. 119.

26. Quoted in Larson, *Bound for the Promised Land*, p. 94.

27. Quoted in Bradford, *Harriet Tubman*, p. 39.

28. Benjamin Quarles, "Harriet Tubman's Unlikely Leadership," in Leon Litwack and August Meier, eds., *Black Leaders of the Nineteenth Century*. Urbana: University of Illinois Press, 1988, p. 49.

29. Quoted in Bordewich, *Bound for Canaan*, p. 355.

30. Quoted in Humez, *Harriet Tubman*, pp. 290–91.

31. Quoted in Humez, *Harriet Tubman*, p. 292.

32. Quoted in Bradford, *Harriet Tubman*, p. 62.

Chapter Four:
"The Slaves Call Her Moses"

33. Quoted in Blockson, *The Underground Railroad*, p. 171.

34. Quoted in Humez, *Harriet Tubman*, p. 260.

35. Quoted in Humez, *Harriet Tubman*, p. 261.

36. Quoted in Clinton, *Harriet Tubman*, p. 91.

37. Quoted in Humez, *Harriet Tubman*, p. 262.

38. Quoted in Blockson, *The Underground Railroad*, p. 120.

39. Quoted in Blockson, *The Underground Railroad*, p. 120.

40. Quoted in Blockson, *The Under-*

ground Railroad, p. 121.

41. Quoted in Bordewich, *Bound for Canaan*, p. 352.

42. Clinton, *Harriet Tubman*, p. 114.

43. Quoted in Humez, *Harriet Tubman*, p. 199.

Chapter Five:
"To Take Care of My People"

44. Quoted in Humez, *Harriet Tubman*, p. 260.

45. Quoted in Larson, *Bound for the Promised Land*, p. 204.

46. Quoted in Humez, *Harriet Tubman*, p. 55.

47. Quoted in Clinton, *Harriet Tubman*, p. 168.

48. Quoted in Clinton, *Harriet Tubman*, p. 173.

49. Quoted in Larson, *Bound for the Promised Land*, p. 220.

50. Quoted in Humez, *Harriet Tubman*, p. 109.

51. Quoted in Quarles, "Harriet Tubman's Unlikely Leadership," in Litwack and Meier, eds., *Black Leaders of the Nineteenth Century*, p. 46.

52. Humez, *Harriet Tubman*, p. 95.

53. Quoted in Clinton, *Harriet Tubman*, p. 209.

54. Quoted in Larson, *Bound for the Promised Land*, p. 289.

55. Quoted in Humez, *Harriet Tubman*, p. 122.

56. Quoted in Bradford, *Harriet Tubman*, p. 135.

Timeline

ca. 1820–1822 Born to slaves Ben and Harriet "Rit" Ross in Dorchester County, Maryland.

ca. 1835 Suffers a serious blow to her head from a plantation overseer.

1844 Marries John Tubman, a free black.

1849 Fearing she will be sold into the Deep South following her master's death, Tubman flees to Pennsylvania with the aid of the Underground Railroad.

1850 Returns to Maryland for the first time to help her niece and her family escape; Fugitive Slave Act passed by Congress.

1851 John Tubman refuses to accompany Harriet north.

1854 Conducts three of her brothers out of Maryland in a perilous Christmas Day escape.

1857 Assists her aged parents in fleeing Maryland, escorting them all the way to Saint Catharines, Canada.

1858 Meets the controversial freedom fighter John Brown.

1859 John Brown's raid on the federal arsenal in Harpers Ferry, Virginia, ends in failure; Tubman settles her elderly parents in New York State after purchasing property in the town of Auburn.

1860 Helps rescue fugitive slave Charles Nalle in New York and makes final trip for Underground Railroad to Maryland, having by this time led an estimated one hundred slaves to freedom in the North.

1861–1865 During the Civil War travels south to aid the Union cause as a spy, scout, nurse, and cook; in 1863 organizes and helps lead an armed raid up the Combahee River into rebel-held territory in South Carolina.

1869 Marries Civil War veteran Nelson Davis; Sarah Bradford's biography of Tubman is published.

1888 Nelson Davis dies.

1890s Becomes increasingly active in the women's rights movement, speaking at numerous suffrage gatherings in New York and New England.

1896 Purchases property near her house to establish a charitable home for elderly, impoverished, and disabled African Americans.

1908 The Harriet Tubman Home opens in Auburn under the direction of the African Methodist Episcopal Zion Church.

1913 Dies on March 10 of pneumonia and is buried in her adopted hometown of Auburn.

For Further Reading

Books

Judith Bentley, *Harriet Tubman*. New York: Franklin Watts, 1990. A well-researched and highly readable account of Tubman's life and times for young people.

David W. Blight, ed., *Passages to Freedom: The Underground Railroad in History and Memory*. Washington, DC: Smithsonian, 2004. Written for a general audience, this richly illustrated volume covers virtually every aspect of the Underground Railroad, including the land and sea routes, the hiding places, and the best-known conductors and stationmasters such as Harriet Tubman and William Still.

Charles L. Blockson, *Hippocrene Guide to the Underground Railroad*. New York: Hippocrene, 1994. Part travel guide and part reference book, this fascinating work describes the private homes, churches, businesses, and other buildings used as stations or safe houses on the Underground Railroad as well as providing biographical sketches of leading Railroad agents.

———, *The Underground Railroad: Dramatic Firsthand Accounts of Daring Escapes to Freedom*. Upper Saddle River, NJ: Prentice Hall, 1987. Compelling and moving, these firsthand accounts by fugitive slaves testify to the courage, ingenuity, and resolve of the men and women who risked their lives to reach freedom on the Underground Railroad.

Sarah Bradford, *Harriet Tubman: The Moses of Her People*, 1886. Reprint, New York: Carol, 1994. Written during the famous Underground Railroad conductor's lifetime, this biography is based largely on the author's conversations with Tubman.

Gena K. Gorrell, *North Star to Freedom: The Story of the Underground Railroad*. New York: Delacorte, 1997. This richly illustrated history of the Underground Railroad for young people includes a discussion of the many challenges that fugitive slaves confronted after they reached freedom.

Stuart A. Kallen, *Life on the Underground Railroad*. San Diego: Lucent, 2000. A clearly written and well-organized account of the men and women who participated in the Underground Railroad, including stationmasters, conductors, and the fugitive slaves themselves.

M.W. Taylor, *Harriet Tubman: Antislavery Activist*. Philadelphia: Chelsea House, 1991. This generously illustrated juvenile biography includes detailed discussions of Tubman's relationship with abolitionist John Brown and contributions to the Union effort during the Civil War.

Web Sites

Harriet Tubman.com (www.harriettub man.com). Sponsored by the Harriet Tubman Historical Society, this site features the society's extensive collection of articles, photos, programs, and official documents recognizing Tubman's many accomplishments and contributions.

Harriet Tubman: Moses of Her People (http://womenshistory.about.com/library/ weekly/aa020419a.htm). Includes a good biographical sketch of Tubman, a list of books for further study, and contemporary photos.

New York History Net: The Life of Harriet Tubman (www.nyhistory.com/ harriettubman/life.htm). This short biography includes useful discussions of Tubman's role in the Underground Railroad and her life in Auburn, New York.

The Underground Railroad (www. nationalgeographic.com/railroad/j2. html). Designed for young people, this interactive site imaginatively re-creates a perilous Underground Railroad journey from Maryland to the free North led by Harriet Tubman herself.

Index

abolitionist lecture circuit, 71–73
abolitionist movement, 43
abroad marriages, 16–17
agriculture, changing nature of, 24, 26–27
Alabama, 27
Andrew, John, 77, 83
Anthony, Susan B., 90
Anti-Slavery Society, 44
auction block, 24

beatings, 20–21
birth dates, 12, 14
birth location, 13–14
black soldiers, 79–80, 83–84
Bordewich, Fergus, 42
Bowley, John, 48, 50
Bowley, Kessiah, 48, 50
Bradford, Sarah, 20, 42, 47, 85, 87, 88
Brinkley, William, 44, 45
Brodess, Edward, 15, 16, 27, 32, 36
  death of, 38–39
  hiring-out by, 19, 29
Brodess, Eliza, 38, 48, 51
Brodess, Mary Pattison. See Thompson, Mary Brodess
Brown, William Wells, 72
Buffalo, New York, 55
Burris, Samuel D., 44

Canada, rescue missions to, 52–55
cargo, 43
charitable work, 90–91
Cheney, Ednah, 65, 66, 67
childhood, 8, 15–24
children, 35
  hiring-out of, 18–19
  slave, 15–16

Christianity, 62–65
Civil War
  black soldiers in, 79–80, 83–84
  Tubman during, 11, 76–84
  veterans, 84, 88
  see also Combahee River raid
Clinton, Catherine, 11, 15, 70
Combahee River raid, 11, 80–83
conductors, 43
Cook, James, 19
corn crops, 26
cotton gin, 27
cotton plantations, 27
courage, 62–63

daguerreotypes, 64
Davids, Tice, 40
Davis, Nelson, 87–88
death, 92–93
Deep South, 27, 39
Dorchester County, 32–33, 51–52
Douglass, Frederick, 14, 49, 52, 53, 93
Drew, Benjamin, 28

Emancipation Proclamation, 79–80
escape
  dreams of, 36–38
  plans, 39–42
  Tubman's, 42–45
ex-slaves, on the Underground Railroad, 10

fatigue, 32
fieldwork, 30
Fifteenth Amendment, 90
Fifty-fourth Regiment, 83
financial problems, 85–87
Florida, 27

Fort Monroe, Virginia, 84
Fort Wagner, 83
free blacks, 34–35, 40–41
free-slave marriages, 35
Fugitive Slave Act, 10
Fugitive Slave Law, 52–55
fund-raising efforts, 71–73

Garrett, Thomas, 56, 58–59, 61, 62
Georgia, 27
Gibbs, Jacob, 48
grain agriculture, 26

Harriet Tubman (Bradford), 88
Harriet Tubman Home, 90–92
head wound, 31–32
Higginson, Thomas Wentworth, 72–73
hiring-out system, 17–19
Humez, Jean, 90

Incidents in the Life of a Slave Girl (Jacobs),
    37
injuries, 31–32
Isaac, James, 52

Jacobs, Harriet, 37

Larson, Kate Clifford, 16, 18
Lincoln, Abraham, 76, 79–80, 83
Louisiana, 27

marriages, 35
    abroad, 16–17
    of Tubman, 33–35, 39–40, 51–52,
        87–88
Maryland, 24, 41
military hospitals, 85
Mills, Polish, 23
Mississippi, 27
musical code, 68

Nalle, Charles, 73–74
Narrative of the Life of Frederick Douglass
    (Douglass), 14
Nat Turner's Rebellion, 24, 25

nerves, 66–67, 69
New Jersey, 43
North, the, 43, 85
nursing experiences, 83–84, 85

packages, 43
passengers, 43
Pattison, Athon, 35–36
Pennsylvania, 47–48
Pennsylvania Society for the Abolition of
    Slavery, 56
personality strengths, 66–67, 69
Philadelphia, Pennsylvania, 47–48
Port Royal Island, 77–79
postwar discrimination, 85
punishments, 10
    of recaptured slaves, 9, 38

Quarles, Benjamin, 56

rebellious streak, 23
religious faith, 62–65
rescue missions, 62
    to Canada, 52–56
    of family members, 47–48, 50 52,
        59 61, 74
    Nalle rescue and, 73–74
    of parents, 69–70
    planning of, 65–66
    precautions on, 66–67
Ross, Ben (father), 14, 15, 16, 32, 61
    rescue of, 69–70
Ross, Benjamin (brother), 38–42, 59–61
Ross, Harriet (mother), 13, 15, 16, 23
    controversy over Pattison's will and,
        35–36
    rescue of, 69–70
Ross, Henry (brother), 38–42, 59–61
Ross, Linah (sister), 27–28, 36
Ross, Moses (brother), 51
Ross, Soph (sister), 27–28, 36
runaway attempts, 20–21
runaway slaves, 57
    numbers of, 9, 46
    punishments faced by, if caught, 9, 38

Sanborn, Franklin B., 21, 32, 83
Scenes in the Life of Harriet Tubman (Bradford), 87
Seward, William H., 70–71
siblings, 15, 27–28
slave children, 15–16
slave families, 16
    effect of hiring-out system on, 18–19
    separations faced by, 27–28
slave labor, 27
    hiring out, 17–19
slave marriages, 16–17
slave memoirs, 37
slave parents, difficulties faced by, 15–16
slave patrols, 23–24
slave revolt, 24, 25
slaves, 12, 35
    fears of, of being sold, 24, 26–28, 39
slave trade, 27
South Carolina, 27
spirituals, as secret code, 68
spying activities, 80–83
stationmasters, 43
stations, 43
Stewart, John, 32, 43
Still, William, 56–57, 58
suffragist movement, 88–90

teenage years, 29–33
theatrics, 69
Thompson, Anthony C., 14, 15, 38

Thompson, Mary Brodess, 14, 15, 16
tobacco plantations, 24, 26
Truth, Sojourner, 86
Tubman, Harriet
    dreams of freedom by, 36–38
    faith of, 62–65
    government treatment of, 84
    as hired out labor, 17–21, 29–33
    loss of sisters by, 27–29
    personality of, 23, 66–67, 69
    return home by, 51–52
Tubman, John, 33–35, 39–40, 51–52, 87
Turner, Nat, 24, 25

Underground Railroad, 8, 9, 40, 43
    Tubman as conductor on, 10–11, 46–61
    Tubman's escape on, 8–9, 42–45
Underground Railroad, The (Still), 57

veteran pensions, 84, 88
Virginia, 24

Washington, Booker T., 92
wheat crops, 26
whites, fears of, of slave insurrection, 23–24
Whitney, Eli, 27
women's rights movement, 88–90
work-for-hire arrangement, 32

Picture Credits

About the Author

Louise Chipley Slavicek received her master's degree in American history from the University of Connecticut. Her books for young people include *Women of the American Revolution, Bloody Mary,* and *Life Among the Puritans.* She lives in central Ohio with her husband, Jim, a research biologist, and their two children, Krista and Nathan.